A Child Born with Sickle Cell
The Untold Secret

By: Lamour Bluitt

"Push yourself, because no one is going to do it for you."
- Unknown

"Take a deep breath, look you are alive."
- Lamour Bluitt

Overview and Vocabulary

Sickle cell disease encompasses a group of disorders where red blood cells assume a sickle shape, leading to early cell death and a shortage of healthy red blood cells (Sickle cell anemia). This can result in the blockage of blood flow causing painful episodes known as Sickle cell crises.

Symptoms:
The symptoms include infections, pain, and fatigue. These may manifest as sudden chest or joint pain, dizziness, fatigue, and abnormal breakdown of red blood cells, among others.

Treatments:
Treatment options include medications, blood transfusions, and, in rare cases, bone-marrow transplants. Medications used are Narcotics, Chemotherapy, Vitamins, and Blood transfusions.

Specialists:
Specialists involved in the treatment include Hematologists, Cardiologists, Pulmonologists, Neurologists, Pediatricians, Primary Care Providers (PCP), and Emergency medicine doctors.

Signs and Symptoms:
Symptoms of sickle cell anemia range from anemia, episodes of pain, painful swelling of hands and feet, frequent infections, delayed growth, vision problems, and low oxygen levels contributing to various symptoms.

Effects of Environmental Factors:
Sickle cell disease can worsen under extreme conditions such as high altitude, dehydration, illness, stress, sleep apnea, menstruation, exposure to cold temperatures, and intense exercise.

Complications and Risks:
Complications of sickle cell anemia can lead to various health issues such as strokes, acute chest syndrome, pulmonary hypertension, and organ damage. Moreover, certain risk factors increase the chances of a baby being born with sickle cell anemia.

Types of Sickle Cell Disease:
Different types of Sickle Cell Disease include HbSs, HbS beta thalassemia, and rarer forms like HbSD, HbSE, and HbSO.

Acknowledgment

I extend my heartfelt gratitude to the Mayo Clinic and its dedicated doctors and healthcare professionals for their invaluable medical insights and support. Special thanks to the various specialists, including Hematologists, Cardiologists, Pulmonologists, and many others, for their contributions.

I am indebted to my family from the Bluitt, Johnson, and Clayton communities, who have been my unwavering pillars of strength. I express my deepest appreciation to my sisters Ivy C. Bluitt and Ollienna A. Bluitt for their guidance and wisdom during their struggles with sickle cell disease.

I am eternally grateful for the unwavering support of my friends and mentors, especially Robert Richie and Kiernan Richardson, Anthony Macio Gordon, David Kimba for their continual encouragement and assistance. The friends list goes on. A special mention to my father Stanley Lamar Bluitt, my mother Zephreda Dumas Bluitt, for their love and unwavering support.

I would like to acknowledge the University of Iowa Hospitals & Clinics for their exceptional care and service, as well as the Iowa City community for their continuous support. My heartfelt thanks to the Amazon Kindle Publishing community for their unwavering support and opportunities.

I also extend my gratitude to all the mentors, entrepreneurs, business owners, and partners who have contributed to my journey. My appreciation to the Merge for the IC colab and the Prairie Lights Bookstore for their support. I am grateful to social media platforms for providing a space for entrepreneurs and business owners to reach a wider audience.

Last but not least, my heartfelt appreciation goes out to the Merge community in Iowa City 1 Million Cups for their continued support and encouragement.

Dedication

This book is dedicated to my beloved sister Ollienna A. Bluitt, a resilient survivor of sickle cell disease. Your beauty, compassion, and understanding inspire me every day. Keep shining with that genuine smile. I love you dearly.

To my sister Ivy C. Bluitt, a remarkable mother of four, a strong leader, and a role model for resilience in the face of sickle cell anemia. Your enduring strength and determination are a testament to your extraordinary spirit. I love you sis!

I extend my dedication to all the children who bravely endure the challenges of sickle cell disease from the moment of their birth. To the families, parents, and patients fighting alongside them, your strength is admirable. You are all beautiful and resilient, holding onto hope in the face of adversity.

A heartfelt tribute to the professors and teachers in Chicago, Illinois, and the health experts and specialists in the Iowa City community.

To the esteemed professors at the University of Iowa College of Medicine, the dedicated doctors, nurses, and all other professionals, your unwavering support and expertise are deeply appreciated.

Chapter 1

In the summer of 1996, in the month of August, a child was born at the Michael Reese Hospital in Chicago, Illinois. Kim Davis, the newborn, brought tears of joy to her parents, Debra and Sam Davis. However, their happiness was marred by the news that Kim would have to stay in the hospital for a few days for further examination. Debra, having endured thyroid cancer, exhibited an inherited trait that had been passed down her bloodline, causing concern and worry among the family.

Despite the challenges, the family found solace in their togetherness, sharing moments of nostalgia and comfort in their modest home. Amidst the city's trials and tribulations, they awaited Kim's discharge, excited to bring her home to a new crib and a loving environment.

Their joy was momentarily shattered when they received a call from the hospital. The news that Kim had been born with sickle cell anemia sent shockwaves through the family, prompting tears and concerns for their newborn. Nevertheless, they were assured that Kim was otherwise healthy, and the family rushed to the hospital to bring their baby home.

Once back home, the family settled into a routine, with Debra breastfeeding Kim and Sam providing unwavering support. Kim, a content and peaceful baby, filled their home with joy and laughter, bringing warmth to their hearts.

The nurses gave Debra and her husband Sam a phone call. "Ring ring" the phone rings. The nurse quietly responds, "Hey Debra. I hope all is well with you. We saw something abnormal with your baby that she has been diagnosed with sickle cell disease from a blood test." Kim Davis was only a few weeks from being born and coming home from the Michael Reese Hospital in Chicago, Illinois. Debra Davis, who is the mother of Kim, Sam Davis, who is Kim's biological father were gathering around the bed with such happiness, tears in their eyes of the delivery with their beautiful child.

Debra had suffered from thyroid cancer which caused her neck to swell and grow the size of a cantaloupe. Causing disruptive swelling in the neck, that made her eyes big. It was hereditary spread from generation to generation leading the trait down the bloodline. Kim was eight pounds when she was born a pretty healthy baby. "My baby is so precious just look at her sleep peacefully" as Sam mentions to Debra "Yes I know honey she is adorable!"

Walking the southside streets of Chicago an older lady got her purse snatched from a homeless guy. Debra looked out the window from the hospital room where she had her labor giving birth to her child Kim. "Look!" The nurses rushed over to the window to see what Debra was all surprisingly shocked about. "Some guy just robbed that poor old lady; this is just insane." "Wow, that is not good!" The nurse says shockingly "Why would that guy rob that old lady?" "I guess it's only when times are really hard." "He is homeless!" Sam says aggressively out of sarcasm "Oh that answers my question." "Karma will get a hold of him either way regardless." The nurse says with such humor.

Loud thunder and rain while the family gathered their belongings getting ready to head out to go home. Knowing they're precious, the baby girl will be discharged from the hospital tomorrow morning. They went and had dinner watching Good Times on the old television that they've had since the late 80's. "This is our favorite show we used to watch back in the day, do you remember honey?" Debra excitedly asked Sam "Yes I do remember." "Brings back such great memories when you and I first met over at the old Cubs Wrigley field stadium near the North and Westside of Chicago." Eating some of the best Chicago style butter popcorn with caramel, drinking soda sitting relaxing on the brown sofa in their two-bedroom apartment. The Davis family had just bought a new sofa set, dining room set with the matching table cloth on top, had brand new cabinets replaced due to the mold in the kitchen that causes bacteria and sickness. Baby crib for Kim when she comes home, two new lamps for the living room and a fireplace set they got from the antique store The Printed Lady located on 1819 W Grand Ave.

The space there is impeccable and when it comes to satisfying their customers, they really care about making their people happy, comfortable, and providing the best quality antique furniture in the Midwest. Kim's parents got ready for the big exciting day of picking their child up from the hospital. "I'm so excited Kim is about to finally come to her new crib, this means so much." As Debra was walking around looking for her purse "Yes, I cannot wait any longer for my baby!" Sam says deliberately. "Okay, I've found what I was looking for now, I'm ready to go." Debra and Sam were getting ready to get Kim from the hospital as the cell phone rang. Ring, ring, ring, it was the nurse "Hello! May I ask who's calling?" Debra says surprisingly! "It's Nicole the nurse over at Michael Reese hospital I just wanted to share some news with you guys on Kim." "She's really healthy although she was born with sickle cell anemia as our lab specialist diagnosed her, which will be her second blood test and the results got back to us quickly. I will explain more when you guys arrive." Debra glanced over at Sam, her husband and started crying and getting worried "What's wrong honey?" Sam says. "I'm ok, just kind of sad and concerned that our child has been born with sickle cell disease." Debra says "Is she alright?" "How is she doing?" Sam asked out of curiosity. "Yes, she's healthy, the nurse says and they will elaborate with us more when we arrive." "Okay that's fine!" As Sam got less anxious.

  They have now arrived over at the hospital and rushed to get inside to get their baby. She was sleeping peacefully and had long hair; her skin was as rich brown as drinking a fresh glass of almond chocolate milk. "There's my beautiful baby girl." Sam says excitedly, removing the sheet from over Kim. "I'm really happy honey!" "God is good to us all of the time." Debra looked at the nurse standing in the room with her clipboard and said thank you! "I just wanted to thank you so much and the other doctors, nurses and you all are really a blessing for the successful delivery of our new born child and the help that you all provided for me and my family." Thank you." "No problem at all you guys truly deserve our attention and support," From the nurse. Nicole walked into the room and ran to Debra and out of generosity hugged her extremely tight with love, care, and gratitude. "God bless you and your family for anything don't hesitate to call; as= a matter of fact here's my personal contact number of where you can reach me."

  Nicole handed over a card to Debra, her main emergency contact. "I cannot thank you enough, you guys truly are amazing and very supportive." "Thank you!" "Enjoy the rest of your day" as Debra, Kim, and Sam was off to home. "We made it!" "Oh honey can you make sure that Kim has her milk or as in fact, I made a commitment to breast feeding our baby instead." "Believe it's best for her to drink and eat naturally." "Sounds important!" Sam was taking off his shoes when they arrived at their place. Debra went into the living room; as she placed Kim's blanket across her chest and placed the other pink and white blanket around her while breastfeeding. "Are you hungry?" Sam asked Debra. "I'm fine as of right now, thank you anyways babe." "Kim needs to eat more to keep her bones strong and healthy." "Yes, I agree that's why I love you so much for understanding." Kim sleeps drinking from her mother's breast, Debra rubs Kim's hair explaining her love she has for her husband Sam unconditionally.

"I love you more honey, and our beautiful baby girl." Sam says genuinely. "Tomorrow morning, I will go buy groceries." Debra says... "We have to go get some catfish from the meat market. I want to make some fried catfish with salad and garlic bread for dinner." "That does sound delicious making my mouth water as we speak" Sam started to laugh, chuckled a little bit. Kim is such a good baby she rarely cries and is quiet most of the time." "Can you pass me Kim's bib honey from off the table please?" Debra says to her husband Sam, "yes I may; are you about to burp her?" Sam mentions, "yes it's about that time she's all full!" Debra says while holding Kim on her shoulder as she softly burps her. Burb! Kim releases great energy by getting fussy, and quite aggravated when she is sleepy. Although, she would not cry as much as a normal baby would. Kim is a pretty chilled, laidback happy baby with a great sense of humor and smile.

Chapter 2

A famous quote by Lamour Bluitt, "If you change your surroundings, you change your life," echoed through Debra, Sam, and Kim's journey to Texas to attend the funeral of Debra's beloved uncle Joe, a former United States Navy SEAL and esteemed journalist. Uncle Joe's battle with post-traumatic stress disorder had left a lasting impact on the family, underscoring the importance of mental health awareness. Despite the somber occasion, the family found solace in the warm embrace of their extended relatives in Arlington, Texas. Mrs. Patty, a comforting presence, welcomed them with open arms, fostering a sense of togetherness and support during their time of grief.

Amidst the reminiscing and shared memories, the family was introduced to the vibrant community of Arlington, with its thriving university and bustling cultural landmarks. The Texas weather greeted them warmly, setting the stage for a heartfelt reunion. As they prepared for Uncle Joe's funeral, the emotional atmosphere hung heavy in the air, permeated with memories and sorrow. Pastor Cliff's heartfelt prayer offered solace and comfort to the grieving family, as they bid farewell to their beloved Uncle Joe.

The graveside ceremony evoked a flood of emotions as the family paid their last respects, honoring Uncle Joe's legacy and service. Tears flowed freely as they laid him to rest, surrounded by poignant tributes and symbols of his military service.

Kim woke up crying screaming at the top of her lungs as if she was being abused or having a nightmare. "Please baby may you stop at the nearest gas station so we can see what's wrong with Kim!" As Debra reaches in the back seat, picking her up gently as Sam pulls over into the gas station right by the highway. Debra says to Sam "I believe her body is hurting her. I've noticed lately ever since Kim has been home, she has not been the same." "I've noticed Kim was getting 10-12 hours of sleep, poor ability to stay unassisted (Suggested to use a wheelchair), inability to have treatments and blood transfusion. Frequency about 4 weeks (1 month)." "This is quite scary! I will do my very best to stay strong and leave it all to God's control." Debra was sad, depressed and felt awful sobbing of her and Sam child Kim going into a crisis. The family had finally arrived in the Texas city of Arlington, west of Dallas. The weather was 67 degrees F (19 degrees C). With wind S at 17 MPH (27 km/h), 85% humidity.

Happy and excited to see each other for such decades the family of three generations reunite and share the love introducing Debra, Sam, and baby Kim to Arlington, Texas its home to the University of Texas at Arlington (UTA), Whose campus has a modera planetarium. In River Legacy Parks, trails cut through hardwood forest rich in wildlife. The park also has the River Legacy Living Science Center, with aquariums, terrariums and interactive exhibits. The Dallas Cowboys football team plays at AT&T Stadium, which also hosts concerts. "I'm so glad to see you give me a hug girl." Mrs. Patty says to Debra as she hugs her tight. "Same here how have you been? And you still look good!" Debra says to Mrs. Patty, kissing her on the cheek. "I've been blessed with getting the family ready for your great uncle's funeral. I'm keeping all of his old belongings with me wherever I go." Mrs. Patty says diligently. "Where's Sam and baby Kim?" "They're right outside talking to Leon." Debra says looking out of the window. "Hold up, let me go get them, I'll be right back."

Debra walks out the door to get Kim and Sam trying not to disturb his conversation with Leon." "Excuse me for one second Leon, I want to show Mrs. Patty the baby." As Debra walks back inside of the house. "Mrs. Patty, I have a surprise for you, look who said hi." "Oh, look at her beautiful self she is adorable just like her mother." Mrs. Patty with a big smile on her face of happiness and joy. "Thank you!" "Yes, she is a charm, the only problem is that my baby is diagnosed with sickle cell disease." Debra sadly elaborated with Mrs. Patty about Kim's sickness. "She has a very painful disability. The doctor said as she gets older I should follow up with a strict diet for her, help her with the proper breathing techniques, staying active with doing the things she loves rather than hobbies, routines, and or adventures. I want her to understand that Kim is no longer different from any other child normally, or with a disability. They are all smart, intellectual, intelligent, and unique in their own way."

Mrs. Patty was looking at Debra as she explained children with disabilities are normal. "Yes, I agree dear although I and the family are happy to see you all." Mrs. Patty pats Debra on the shoulder as she gives a soft hug. "Thank you for your understanding, always there for me." Debra says to Mrs. Patty. "No problem family and please don't worry yourself Kim is a healthy baby. Bless and protect!" Says Mrs. Patty to Debra. Knocking appeared at the door "knock, knock, knock!" A guy appeared in a black and red suit with a black tie who

who was related to Debra. "He is clean; look at him always styling shoes to match the shirt, shirt has to match the socks." With laughter Mrs. Patty says. "That's your third-generation cousin; that you never met. I'm sure he has some type of great career, job, and or business.

He is so intelligent that he went to college to get his (MBA) Master Bachelor Associates." As Mrs. Patty was about to talk. Debra ear's off here comes Sam whistling energetically. "Hey, hey how is my beautiful family? I'm such a great spirit." Sam says to his wife Debra and Mrs. Patty. "That's a great thing which is a blessing baby. How is everyone out front doing?" Says Debra to Sam. "They are all good! We talked for a minute, just chatting about investing into the markets you know real estate, assets, merchandise." Sam explains to Debra. "It's about that time baby! Really it is I have our daughter Kim which is my little soul, and angel. I have you, my beautiful, gorgeous wife! It's that time." Sam with a serious look in his eye, then walked into the kitchen to grab some water from the refrigerator. "I'm thirsty, do you guys want anything to drink?" Sam speaks to Debra and Mrs. Patty. Drastically the family of three Debra, Sam, and Kim for a funeral that was in the morning. "We're planning to leave right after the funeral. So Kim can take her treatment that they forgot to pack in the suitcase. Have to get my baby home just in case her body starts to hurt." Debra says historically.

It was raining outside on a Sunday morning, the snow storm was supposed to bypass West of Dallas Texas heading East mix weather of rain, sleet, and snow. The family was getting ready for the funeral of their great uncle; it was the wake first, then the actual service. As the family waits for the limo to arrive Debra walks into the living room where her cousin was in the corner crying and sobbing due to their uncle's death. Debra walked up to the girl and asked her what's wrong and will she be able to stand up. "Are you okay? Would you like to ride with me in the limousine?" Debra asks nicely and gracefully. "Is it okay if you stand? I don't want you laying on the floor in the corner all alone. We are here together. I'm sorry I know you were really close to him." Debra said while taking a deep breath. "Okay guys, the limo is here, are you ready? Let's go praise God!" Mrs. Patty kept the family together for three generations with the last name Smith. Until Debra married her husband Sam Davis. "Off in the limo we go!" Screams Debra.

The family is on their way to the funeral for the broken-hearted relations that were close to their great uncle. The family of Smith's third generation was packed with a lot of people even though some of his college buddies were at the funeral. Bunch of people came to say their last goodbyes and condolences; very emotional energy was in the atmosphere and it was filled with love, support, grief and gratitude. Meeting and greeting with other family members, friends, colleagues, foe or whatever the relationship status is it was like a mini reunion. Genuine attitudes especially the ones that didn't see each other for a very long time or just never met in general. Before the pastor came out to give his service preaching the good gospel, people kept arriving, showing that the room was full with 300 people in total. "Now, let us all have a seat."

Chapter 3

As the family bid farewell to their Texas relatives, they made their way back to Chicago, carrying with them the warmth and memories of their time spent together. Debra and Sam reminisced about the joyful moments shared with their extended family, finding solace in the love and support they had experienced during their visit. Returning home, the couple prepared for their daughter Kim's first birthday celebration. Excitedly planning a small gathering at Chuck E. Cheese's, they looked forward to making Kim's special day memorable and joyful.

At the arcade, Kim's gleeful reactions to the music and festivities filled Debra and Sam's hearts with joy. They marveled at Kim's exuberant response to the lively atmosphere, envisioning a bright and promising future for their little one. Amidst the celebrations, Debra unexpectedly encountered her old high school classmate Monica, who shared news of her own children and career achievements. The reunion added a nostalgic touch to the day, creating a bridge between the past and the present.

The heartfelt rendition of "Happy Birthday" by Monica's children, TJ and Tasha, brought an added layer of warmth and joy to the celebration, further cementing the precious memories of the day in Debra and Sam's hearts. On the way home, amidst the silence of the journey, Debra found herself lost in thought, reliving the day's events and basking in the joy of Kim's milestone birthday. Sam, preparing for a job interview in the construction field, reflected on the day's experiences and the blessings that surrounded their family.

The family gathers their belongings getting ready to head out back towards Chicago. Midwest off they go, "Kim is almost one year old." Goodbye everyone and it was a pleasure seeing, staying with you all really made us feel like home." Debra says genuinely to her family. "Thank you! It was an honor. I enjoy all your company, the fact I'm really going to miss my baby Kim" Mrs. Patty says. Goodbye now!" Sam, Debra, and baby Kim went off from Dallas Texas heading back to Chicago. "What did you think, honey?! Did you enjoy yourself at least despite the funeral?" Debra asks her husband Sam out of curiosity. "Yes I had a great time and meeting your uncle's, aunties, and cousins was just fantastic!" Laughing historically to himself says Sam. "Good! I'm glad that you enjoyed yourself, especially my crazy family. That's always a plus." Debra kisses her husband Sam on the cheek with love and care. Getting back on schedule with things work and all the family had to make sure that Kim had a babysitter, until Debra became a stay at home mom. While Sam remains the breadwinner; Kim's birthday is tomorrow turning one years old.

They went out to get her some strawberry, chocolate cake with pink frosting matching her pink and white brand new outfit that her parents bought for her. Instead of having a party for Kim, the family just decided to take her to Chuck E. Cheeses to listen to the music while Chucky and the band performed. Again Debra and Sam thought to themselves that Kim is only turning one by the time Kim turns 3 years old she will have the birthday that she could possibly imagine at the age of three. "We're going to stop home for a bit to check on the place then, we can head back out! I'm thinking of ordering, creating her a cake from Jewel Osco? How does that sound?" Debra asked Sam with a smile on her face. "Yes, that would be perfectly fine with me." Sam points at the cake. "I believe I've got to grab some ice cream!" Debra says out of laughter. "That does sound good, Kim is just a baby missing out!" "Hahaha" Sam and his wife Debra laugh spontaneously out loud.

"Yes I agree honey baby Kim has a long way to go...that's okay my little precious baby mommy got you a cake, that I will allow you to taste just a little tiny bit only cause I'm so happy." Debra told Sam that she would place frosting on the baby spoon so that Kim will only taste a little bit of flavor. "She's only one darling!" Sam explains to his wife Debra placing his hand on top of her hand. "That may be too much sugar and sweets for her, don't you think so? I mean I guess just a little tiny bit." Sam is looking at Kim. "Don't worry honey I will only give her a little bit." Debra says to Sam with a serious demeanor. "I can't wait to see baby Kim's face. It would be the most beautiful moment ever. Debra says happily. "She is a happy baby with such humor that attracts people, animals...hey whomever that gets to be near her. Will be happy!" Debra looks over at her husband Sam.

Sam and Debra arrive at the grocery store to put in an order for Kims cake, where they both are having a conversation on what Kim would love when she gets older, a lot like the other kids, in which they understand that people are different and they have their own style, taste in things. Rather it's toys, movies, music, television shows, books, clothes, shoes, possibly anything that you could think of what other children love as they get older to start realizing and what keeps them happy. "Now, that would be the moment." Debra looks at the window. It's kind of overrated that everyone loves the same thing that has a logo, brand or is popular at the moment." Debra says jokingly but somewhat seriously. "All we have to do is wait and see! And let Kim decide what she loves. Just because she has pink and white in her room; she might love orange." Sam explains theoretically to his wife Debra. They finally get into the section of the store near the bakery section where all the goodies and desserts are near. A scream appeared from the worker/employee. "Hey, take that out of your pocket right now!" Yelling at a customer that got caught stealing some scotch tape. Can I get a manager out in aisle 6!" The employee says in her walkie talkie.

   The manager walked up quickly to where the employer and thief were standing. "What's going on!?" The manager shouts fiercely. "This guy stole some scotch tape! Need to have him arrested off of the premises, I have him on camera as well!" Then, the Chicago police department showed up to take down a report and arrest the robber. Running his name into the computer he is a class X felon, charged with other criminal backgrounds of a robber, burglar, assault on an officer in the past. Aggravated assault on a bus passenger. Sam and Debra grabbed their baby's cake and went off into the aisle where the ice cream was in. "That was crazy honey! People are just ignorant! Robbing and stealing from out of the store, not only robbing old ladies for their purse. Chicago is just insane!" Debra screams out of frustration. "It's about everywhere, it's the people and in the environment." Sam says intelligently to his wife Debra. Don't take it personal, baby; that's just the way it is." Sam says with his hands on his hips. With a look of disgust, irritability, and frustration in Debra's face Sam knew that his wife was ready to leave Chicago. She was getting to her breaking point. Making a picky decision on what ice cream to go with due to all kinds of delicious choices Sam had a taste for some chocolate ice cream; but Debra wanted strawberry and vanilla ice cream. They both came to a decision and got both. "This is going to be extremely delicious with my graham crackers." Says Debra enthusiastically.

   Sam and Debra got what they needed and went into the self-check-out. Sam asked his wife Debra if she got everything that she needed. "You got everything?" "Yes I got what was just perfect to add with baby Kim's cake." Debra said to her husband Sam. On their way home it was very peaceful, with impeccable diligent energy. They made it home and Sam kicked his boots off right at the door. "I know a lady whose son has a chronic disease of neurofibromas skin and sickle cell anemia. He's now 21 years old. He plays football, which I am shocked about because that can also trigger a crisis. Getting tackled hard!

It's sad when she told me that he is always in and out of the hospital." Debra says sadly to her husband Sam. His sickness causes him to go back and forth to the emergency room; his mother says she doesn't think he is always in a serious crisis of pain in which he has pain that we don't experience. Hardly can't get a job due to his sickness, and social security benefits he's receiving from the government. Tracy Jenkins, is his name position is cornerback in football which has been his passion since he was a little boy. I'm sure the exercises he does with the team helps him to keep his heart blood flowing at a fair steady healthy rate. And eating the right healthy foods, at times he goes out with his college friends and has a few drinks out at the bars in Iowa City. Debra speaks sophisticatedly.

His mother seems like a great caring mom for her son. Providing Tracy with that great motherly-love helping, supporting and being there for him while battling with a chronic disease on top of having sickle cell. Making sure that her son balances everything out far as his health. As I was having a talk with Tracy's mother she mentioned that when he was 10-12 years of age his crisis was bad. They did everything that it took for them to cure his disease. Providing him with (OTC) over the counter medicine such as ibuprofen, ibuprofen 800 mg, folic acid hydrocodone, and Xanax. According to Tracy prescription medicine they always provided him with a stronger dose.

Depending on his pain level rated from 1-10, the doctors and nurses knew that it was a serious pain issue, causing excruciating pain in the body. He couldn't function like the normal kids. Keeping him in isolation when it came to being around certain people; distance between the other kids that was having fun without having to go to the hospital. As Tracy got older he fought depression, anxiety and fear. Thinking to himself that he never was going to get healed or restore to be able to live a hospital free life. Which caused separation, devastation and heart brokenness to the family. They did not give up, kept fighting and came up with a solution. Helping him the best way that they possibly can, fortunately, no matter how old Tracy got his family was always supporting him, and he knew that he was really sick with a chronic disease and has sickle cell anemia. "It's based on inheritance and someone in the family has the trait, possibly meaning whoever was to have children will have the illness." Sam says thinking to himself. By the grace of God he has our baby covered and protected. Our father is an almighty God! As long as we believe and have faith we will be alright; Kim would be alright. All of the sick would be in God's hands to restore them, and keep them strong by any means." Aggressively speaking Sam explains to his wife Debra.

"Kim is anointed and born to be active in anything she puts her mind to. Adapting with other kids around her or in life. Living healthy, strong and rich at heart inspiring others around her leaving a message to the world for fighting and continuing to hold on without letting her loved ones down." Sam goes on...leaving tears in his eyes, and his wife's Debra. It was a windy day outside, a sunny afternoon the day of Kim's first birthday where she had turned one year old. The family put up decorations around the place including Kim's room. They headed out to Chuck E. Cheese to take Kim to watch and listen to the band's performance. As they were watching and listening to some great music, Kim was smiling and laughing of joy and happiness along the way. "I think our baby loves music! Sam looked at his wife Debra excitingly. Look how happy she gets especially when music is involved. It was like she understood what type of music that they were performing just at the age of one. My baby is so smart and intelligent!" Debra shouts spontaneously at Sam due to the loud noise in the background of music, people the arcade game rides.

Kids were running and playing everywhere. Just before they started to sing happy birthday and cut the cake, they ate ice cream. Debra saw an old classmate of hers from back in high school. All of a sudden they've made eye-contact and started to meet and greet each other without seeing one another in a very long time. "Hey! How have you've been?" Looking over her shoulders Debra says to her old classmate. "I've been great, now I have my teaching license over at Simeon high school. Just been getting myself prepared for that." Debra's classmate's name is Monica, which they grew up together and shared similar entities. "Where's your little one?!" Debra asks Monica. "I have a 7-year-old and a 9-year-old girl now. Monica says.

"My daughter is 9 and my son is 7. I'm very blessed and happy to be the mother I am to my children. I see that you have yourself a little adorable baby." Monica dramatically says to Debra.

"Yes my baby just turned one year old today," Debra says looking at her daughter Kim. She loves to be out in the world more than in the house all day. hahaha" Debra laughs historically. How long are you guys staying till?" Looking over at Monica; Debra says. "Until 7:30PM CST! I have to get back home and get the kids ready for school and work tomorrow. I started my orientation for my other job." Looking at the big yellow slide Monica says excitedly. "Congratulations! That's great! I am proud of you. Debra says to Monica. Well, you can stay for some cake and ice cream." Monica looked at her phone to check the time. "Perfect, sounds good to me. I will call the kids over to sing happy birthday to Kim. They're so cute. Monica says "Kids!" Come here for a second and meet your auntie and uncle, Cousin Debra, Sam and Kim. Debra is a longtime classmate of mine that I always truly admired. Monica looked over, speaking to her kids. "This is my son TJ. TJ says hi ``"Hello," TJ waves at Debra. And my daughter Tasha. "Hey," Tasha says. "a pleasure to meet y'all." Debra says with happiness and a smile on her face. "It's been that long? Over nine years!" Debra says to Monica.

"Wow! You still look good and God is good! OMG!" This is amazing!" TJ looks over at everyone. Tasha, are you ready to sing happy birthday with me to Kim?" Screams out loud TJ "YES!" Tasha softly says! They gather around one another singing happy birthday. "Happy birthday to you, happy birthday to baby Kim! Happy birthday to you!" Glorious day TJ and his sister Tasha both sang a song to Kim, the most beautiful moment ever for Debra and Sam as well. "Thank you guys so much! You are the best! Says happily Debra. I'm very grateful, and so is my husband Sam. Debra looks to her right and speaks passionately. "This is a very special moment. Never forgotten." Says Debra. The family ended up going their separate ways as Kim's birthday party was over. On their way home Debra was in a deep thought, complete day dream as her mind was in another dimension. Sam was driving and it was silent the whole way. We're they exhausted? Did Debra need a break to gather her thoughts from seeing her old classmates, having a wonderful time with her family at Chuck E. Cheese. "Oh my! Was in deep thought. I'm just happy and satisfied with how today went for Kim's birthday. I really enjoyed myself like I was a kid again hahaha." Debra laughs out loud. Sam walks from out of the back where he was getting dressed to leave for a job interview for a construction company, position as carpenter. He always had experience in that skill as a handyman.

Chapter 4

As the dawn broke on a Monday morning, Sam readied himself for his first day at a prestigious construction company, leaving Debra and their daughter Kim still fast asleep. With a wealth of experience in carpentry, Sam embarked on his new job with a sense of pride and determination, eager to showcase his skills and contribute to the company's projects. Amidst the excitement of his new role, Sam's thoughts often turned to Kim's battle with sickle cell disease, a constant reminder of the delicate balance they needed to maintain for her well-being. Researching tirelessly, Sam sought to find new ways to manage Kim's condition, taking proactive steps to ensure her health and safety.

At the construction company, Sam's skills and expertise were recognized, and he was warmly welcomed into the team, appreciative of the understanding and support they offered regarding his responsibilities as a caregiver for Kim. Back at home, Debra busied herself with household chores and indulged in her favorite novel, finding solace in the story of Malcolm X. Sam's return from work brought a smile to Debra's face, and she eagerly shared the day's events with him, reflecting on the challenges and triumphs of managing Kim's condition.

With plans for a comforting dinner, Sam offered to make a quick trip to the store, ensuring they had the necessary ingredients. Amidst their daily routines, Debra shared her excitement about a work-from-home opportunity, highlighting the flexibility it would offer her in caring for Kim while maintaining her professional career. On his way to the store, Sam's mind wandered to the challenges they faced, contemplating the complexities of finding a cure for Kim's condition and the resilience required to navigate their circumstances. Despite the weight of their struggles, Sam found solace in his faith, acknowledging the protection and guidance they received from a higher power.

The chapter fast-forwards to Kim's eleventh birthday, where she enjoys a day of swimming with friends, only to experience a painful crisis that brings back the reality of her condition. Rushed to the hospital, Kim receives prompt care and reassurance from the medical team, bringing relief to both Debra and Sam. With a mix of emotions, Debra stops by the liquor store to pick up some wine, finding solace in the momentary respite from the day's stresses. Back at home, Sam's thoughtful gesture of putting on one of her favorite movies helps lift Debra's spirits, reinforcing the support and love they shared as a family.

As Kim readies herself for a sleepover, the chapter delves into the challenges she faces as she grapples with the limitations imposed by her condition, highlighting the physical and emotional toll it takes on her young spirit. Despite the difficulties, Kim finds solace in activities like dancing, using them as therapeutic outlets to express herself and find joy amidst the struggles. Waking up getting ready for work early Monday. Made breakfast eggs, bacon, toast and hash brown. Wife Debra and his daughter Kim were still asleep; Sam had his first day at a great billion dollar construction company! As a carpenter with years of experience he's able to build and construct anything. As days go by Sam knows in the back of his mind that his daughter has sickle cell anemia and she can go through a crisis any moment. Managing her diet while she's young helps her as she gets older to balance her chronic disease doing hours of research on restoring this sickness, techniques and methods to obtain an awareness for healing the human body.

"Welcome this is your first day I'm assuming?" Says the lady that works for the company to Sam. "Yes, it is!" Sam said confidently. "How many years of carpentry experience do you have?" Ask the lady of the company. "7 years in Brick Masonry, 4 years in the remodeling business with my dad he was into plumbing as well." Sam says. "That's great, really interesting, well glad to have you a part of the organization." The lady of the company says she is an aggressive businesswoman. Especially when it comes to working with men you have to be firmer and more assertive. Even in most positions above power aggression may show if only necessary. As Sam began to pick up where he'd left off with his carpentry work, he learned a lot more information that was new in Masonry construction. Same old fashion methods, different techniques that would get the job done faster and that's using (AI) artificial intelligence robots that can be controlled hands on or manually most importantly automatic. In this new age artificial intelligence (AI) is taking over jobs, manufacturing labor and mankind in general.

Working on a new upcoming project Sam had to make sure that his daughter Kim and his wife Debra were all set by having a doctor on standby in case Kim was to have a crisis due to sickle cell. He was also aware and knew that his daughter had a chronic illness that may interrupt Sam's work. The good thing is at least his job understands! He was able to take off due to emergency related duties and caregiver, for his daughter Kim. Debra was at home doing some laundry and reading her favorite novel "The Autobiography of Malcolm X" As Told To Alex Haley. Drinking her hot chocolate while Kim was sleeping. Sam arrived home from work with a smile on his face. He said to Debra looking at the mirror on the wall. "Hey honey! I'm so happy that my job loves me and my family already! I put in an early notice and an emergency task on leaving work, or having to take the day off to keep an eye out on Kim. They understand and are ok with that. I will be compensated still." Sam explains to Debra. "That's amazing! Kim is in her room sleeping and as soon as she awakes I will give her food and medicine." Debra walks back into the living room to go sit on the couch. "Sounds great!" Sam says with compassion. "What do you want for dinner?"

    Debra opens the refrigerator and says to Sam. "Broccoli, mashed potatoes, and baked chicken sounds incredible." "Okay it does, we are just out of butter and some of my favorite seasonings." Debra says looking inside of the cabinet. "I'll go to the market and grab some honey, that way you don't have to get Kim ready. She needs the rest." Sams says genuinely to Debra to get his jacket and keys to the vehicle to head out to the store. "Hey baby, when you get back in from the store, I wanted to share more with you on this opportunity that I came across empowering, enriching, educating women to work from home." Debra says sharing exciting news. "Yes, that is a blessing! I can't wait to hear more." With a smile of a Prince charming Sam says. "I got the position to work for a survey base of Team Behavior. Working from home, pretty much anywhere I want." Looking at the television with the remote in her hand flicking through channels. Kim will be right beside me while her dad works during the day." Debra says. I'm just so grateful and extremely blessed that we are anointed and covered." Speaking genuinely from the heart. "Yes I agree honey!" Sam says to his wife Debra. Now I will be back. I'm going to the store to get the seasonings for dinner tonight! I love you!"

    Kissing his wife Debra on the cheek. Sam walked out of the door and was whistling to himself in such a great mood. It was very

very peaceful and you could barely hear the music playing from the radio as Sam was driving alone thinking to himself of how, what, when and where they can find a great strategy to restore his daughter Kim's sickness and chronic disease. By being a strong black man that saw a lot of trauma, and suffered from mental illness he knew that he could not worry himself to death especially when he knows that his baby girl is healthy and protected by the blood of Jesus. His family were pretty religious and spiritual that came together as loving, caring, understanding, genuine with a lot of support, prayed a lot and kept their beliefs plus faith when it came to God's words of wisdom. "I thank you God for protecting not only myself but my family as well. I thank you father for being in my presence when I can count on you! Thank you! Amen."

Before he got out of his car to go into the market Sam silently said a prayer. I needed that powerful self-prayer whew! Such a relief." Sam said out loud with excitement. Then, off he went into the store to do some small shopping for their dinner. As Sam walked into the seasoning aisle, he gave his wife Debra a call. "Hey, honey I'm over at the store now what seasoning did you want me to get specifically?" Sam asked Debra. "Black pepper, red chili, garlic pepper and more herb seasonings." Debra on the phone explaining to her husband Sam. "Amazing baby, sounds incredibly delicious! I'll see you shortly." Sam says hang up the phone. Ten years later, Kim is eleven years old! On a beautiful Tuesday she had gathered with a group of her friends from school, where all 3 girls went swimming at the park district. "We should all go get nachos!" Shouts Melissa Kim friend. "Ok let's go!" "Do you have enough money to cover Becca?" Says Kim to Melissa. "Yes I sure do! Thank God my parents gave me my allowance." Afterwards, the group of friends had snacks and lunch. They had a blast in the pool along with a bunch of other people, it was crowded. Kim couldn't enjoy herself as much as the other kids. Battling with a chronic illness and disease her body caused to go through a crisis, due to the pool water.

For some reason her body hurts when it's cold and going swimming triggers it. She experiences chest pains, back and body aches, extremely painful arms, and leg pains. Being born and diagnosed with sickle cell disease is difficult for most individuals born with this condition. Other people may function normally with or without sickle cell, depending on tolerance level and being able to cope with pain in the joints. Mostly found in the Black community in which genetically spread from one generation to another leaving the one with the trait, give it to his or her child. Kim quickly exits the pool with tears in her eyes. "What's wrong Kim, are you okay?!" Becca shouts out loud. "I'm in pain, my body hurts. I need to call my parents!" Crying with pain, says Kim. "Okay I'm sorry we're calling your mom now!" Panicking in a hurry Kim friends. The phone begins to ring (ring, ring, ring, ring) as Becca and Melissa call Debra for help. Hello, hey Mrs. Debra," Becca says politely with shakiness in her voice. "What's wrong?" Ask Debra. "Kim went through a crisis due to getting in the pool." Becca explains to Kim's mother Debra. "Oh no, let me take her to the hospital!" Debra panicked. "No worries! I need to call my mom!" Becca started crying. Melissa walked up to Becca where she was seated as Melissa grabbed her by the hand and gave Becca a big hug filled with love. The family rushed to Anita hospital emergency clinic. Debra laid Kim across her lap as they had to wait in the waiting room to be seen by a nurse.

Debra began to gently massage Kim's arm until the doctor called their name. "Hmm, mhm, hmmm,mmm." Debra quietly mumbles to herself rocking back and forth rubbing Kim's left arm. "Debra!" As the nurse walked out calling her name. Please follow me." Debra, Kim and the nurse headed in the back room. "How is your daughter?" Ask the nurse. "She is in pain and her crisis has triggered her due to the water at the pool," Debra says. She cannot go swimming because her condition and body is not built for that activity her chest will hurt and more on her body. We must keep her away from the= swimming pools." Debra says with sadness and misery in her voice. "I'm really sorry; that's sad! Doctor Bushra will be with you all shortly!" As the nurse heads out of the room. "Hello, guys, my name is Dr. Bushra! And how can I help you all today?" As Dr. Bushra puts her rubber gloves on, talking to Debra. "My daughter is having a bad crisis, pain that possibly triggered while at the swimming pool with a group of friends. She has sickle cell which causes fatigue, and body ache." "Okay I'm sorry to hear that I will do my very best to help her. What is your daughter's name?" Ask Dr. Bushra. "Kim!" Debra says looking over at her daughter Kim "Kim is a beautiful name!" Dr. Bushra, as she raises the bed. Let me check her temperature."

The doctor grabbed her thermometer and placed it under the tongue, just to one side of the center. Checking Kim's temperature to make sure it was great. Before, doctor Bushra had followed her procedures accordingly. Running tests, diagnosing and doing many operations. "Okay Kim's temperature is perfectly fine. Just continue to give her medicine, feed her fruits." The doctor explained. "This will help keep her system and body healthy, as she gets older, help her understand that staying active and exercising is important, and helps a lot when it comes to dealing with a crisis. She's okay I promise! You have a healthy daughter." Assertive as Dr. Bushra explains to Debra. "Thank you so much Dr. That means a lot!" Breaking down emotionally enthusiast Debra says. "Please keep in touch. I will follow up with you shortly, on scheduling Kim next dr. appointment." Dr. Bushra mentions. "I will do it!" Smiling Debra. They left the doctors on their way home Debra stopped for some wine. Red wine was on her top list having a stressful day; she decided alcohol would ease her pain. She doesn't want Kim taking all of that medicine then painkillers, morphine, hydrocodone, acetaminophen/oxycodone brand name Percocet.

"I'm looking forward to Anita hospital protecting our baby Kim?" As Debra heads towards the liquid store to get some red wine talking to herself; her husband Sam is sitting on the passenger side holding Debra's hand while she drives. Walking inside of the liquor store Debra walks in the wine aisle to get her favorite drink, remaining optimistic about the whole situation that way she can balance through life. Dealing with thyroid cancer, a disease she has herself, and coping with her daughter Kim sickle cell anemia disease. It's complicated and Debra is doing her best with the support of her family, husband and close acquaintances. To continue staying strong for her daughter Kim and husband Sam. "Would that be all for you today ma'am?" The cashier lady opens the register. "Yes that would be all." Debra responds in a sad manner. "Okay great! Your total would be $11.53 cents." Cashier lady reached out to grab the twenty dollar bill from Debra. "Here you go." Debra hands over the money to the cashier lady. "Thank you out of twenty?!" The cashier lady gives Debra her refund amount. Here's an $8.47 change back with a copy of receipt." Yells the cashier lady. As the bagger finishes up with Debra groceries, the bagger asks Debra if she would like her to help her out to her vehicle. "Do you need help getting out of your vehicle?" The bagger asked. "No thank you I got it." Debra said politely with a smile. Off heading home they go. Sam asked Debra if she was doing and feeling okay. He seemed a little worried and curious. "Are you feeling, okay?" Sam asked his wife Debra with a look of concern.

"Yes I'm fine!" Debra responded back to Sam with a demeanor of something that was bothering her uncoincidentally; down and happy at the same time with a gray look in her face of gloominess down and out. They made it home Sam asked Debra if she wanted to watch a movie. He put on one of her favorite throwback, classic bay bay kids movies, pronounced Bebe's Kids a 1992 film. "You know how to make me happy don't you?" With a smile on her face Debra says to her husband Sam. This is my movie! Excitingly out of a burst of joy. Debra's mood went from low to high. May you bring me a glass from the kitchen please?" Sitting comfortably on the couch Debra asked Sam politely. "Yes I will. Do you want your small cup or medium cup?" Sam asked Debra. "Small cup honey." Debra responded. I'm getting it for you right now." Sam says rushing to the kitchen. Bringing over his wife Debra's glass of wine she had a rough day and Sam knows how to make his wife feel great. "Thank you babe! You're the best." Kisses and hugs Debra says to her husband Sam. "No problem, I love you!" And I just want the best for my family." Sam explains to his wife Debra. "I understand that I just let life get the best of me at times! I know I'm blessed! We're blessed!" Debra mentions Sam.

Kim was in her room coloring her nails watching cartoons. She was getting herself ready for a sleepover with friends. Two of her other friends since childhood at age 5; she developed a friendship and a bond at the same time Kim had to isolate at moments having a crisis. Causing her body to hurt and may have to seek a doctor in case of an emergency. Although, paramedics, doctors, and staff all dealt with other individuals with sickle cell. By Kim having sickle cell anemia she can't really do as much as an average person could do! That's simply being in a swimming pool. Due to fatigue she can hardly participate in anything physical. Exercise may help Kim cope through her pain and keep her energized, heart flowing steady, properly. Dancing is another self-therapy that involves rhythm, storytelling and expressing. Kim follows these methods and rituals. I do want you to understand! What would you do if you were in Kim's shoes? Dealing with sickle cell anemia... and a chronic illness disease. Challenge after challenge battling with severe pain, chest pains, muscle aches, excruciating arm pain and being in cold weather due to having low blood cells and not enough oxygenation or iron to the body. Constantly in and out of the hospital; confused, not knowing any solution once so ever. Life is pretty miserable when you're suffering alone. Feeling like nobody's there for you. People rarely went to get a physical for themselves, not along hospital visits. No one really wants to ever have the chance to go see a doctor or visit the emergency hospitals. Individuals that have a sickness and must be hospitalized gets lonely; others don't understand without the illness that those with sickle cell anemia or any other disease suffer more from depression, fatigue, anxiety, suicide thoughts.

Chapter 5

Kim's frustration with her illness surfaces, leading to a heart-to-heart with her parents about the challenges of not feeling like a normal kid. Debra's reassurance and understanding help alleviate Kim's distress, and a spontaneous trip for ice cream lightens the mood, bringing a smile back to Kim's face. As they drive back home, a chance encounter with Kim's former English teacher at the store sparks a brief, nostalgic conversation, reinforcing the sense of community within their neighborhood. Once they drop Kim off for her sleepover, Debra makes an impromptu stop at an artistic collaborative space, immersing herself in the creative energy and finding solace in the vibrant atmosphere.

Meanwhile, Kim enjoys a fun-filled sleepover with her friends, indulging in colorful nail polish choices and playful banter. Amidst the laughter and bonding, the girls decide to call it a night, settling down in Melissa's cozy room. As the night fades into morning, the sound of birds chirping, and the rooster's wake-up call signal the start of a new day. In the early hours, Kim receives a call from her mother, reminding her to take her medication and check-in once she wakes up. Grateful for her mother's vigilance, Kim drifts back to sleep, surrounded by the warmth of her friends' company and the security of her mother's care.

Kim throws her hands up in the air, "I'm frustrated by this sickness that I have. Crossing her arm over another I'm so over the fact that I can't be normal like other kids." Kim cry's sobbing to her parents. "Baby are you alright?!" Debra walks into the kitchen where Kim was standing as Debra slams her keys down on the table. "Baby I want you to feel better and I'm your mother. I'm going to help you." Speaking with a pitch tone in her voice sadly loud. Kim looks at her mother and suddenly, her attitude changes. "Mom, I want to get ice cream please!" Kim desperately asked her mother Debra. "Yes, you may! Smiling at Kim as if her plan worked out in her favor. "Let me grab my keys and we can head out." "Where are you guys going?!" Sam walks into the house; shuts the door. Debra snatched her keys aggressively. "We're heading out for ice cream baby." "Strawberries?!" Sam shouts with humor. Debra and Kim headed out to grab ice cream then, on the way back Kim was being dropped off to her friend's home, for the sleepover. "I'm happy you are feeling better sweetie." Driving while having a conversation with her daughter Kim. "Yes I'm taking my pain like a little champ!" Looking out the window, "Yes I am too; it's a blessing and God gave you strength!" Debra says with genuine confidence. "I love you and dad mom." Kim looks out of the window. "Is it something that you see out of the window outside sweetie? Debra asks Kim with laughter. The little bird flew near the window of Kim where she was in the passenger seat. You are going to be okay!" As it flew away into the cloudy light blue sky.

    The family made it to the store where it seemed overly crowded inside, the checkout line was as long as the NFL football field. Including the self-checkout line that was backed up and some self-checkout were under maintenance issues. Kim saw one of her English teachers from elementary school that had her in quite a shock. Looking over her shoulders out of a sporadic act, the English teacher glanced at Kim and her mother Debra with a look of excitement. "Hey Kim! I'm so happy to see you growing up." Debra points at Kim. "Who is this sweetie?" As Debra asked oddly. Kim chuckled softly. "This is Mr. Art, my elementary 2nd grade teacher mom, don't you remember?" Kim says to her mother Debra. With a shocked look in her eyes. "Oh yes now I do remember! Oh my gosh it's been so long." Reaching to Mr. Art to shake his hand. "Absolutely, how are you Mrs. Davis?" Ask the English teacher. "I'm well, and yourself?" Asked Debra. With his hands in his pocket Mr. Art says. "I am great and abundant. And of course excited to see you guys this is why I love going out in certain places especially locally. Smiling at Kim and Debra. Very purposeful indeed." Debra says. Debra and Kim gave Mr Art a hug. "Just finished gathering a few items and doing some quick shopping." Debra and Kim had to get going now, so Kim can get dropped off at her friend's house for a sleepover."

    Suddenly, Mr. Art quietly walked away. Debra and Kim arrived at Kim's friend's home where she was being dropped off. It was raining hard and loud thunder coming from above the dark, gray gloomy clouds. "I love you honey! Make sure you take your medicine and be sure to call me as soon as you start having pain, and a crisis is coming." Lets the car window down near the passenger side. "I love you more mom! Thank you again." Kim says to Debra out of genuine care. On the way home Debra stopped at a nearby facility...looked like a place where entrepreneurs come to collaborate, and share their creative endeavors. The place was very eccentric, resplendent with an artsy touch to it. There were flat screen televisions across the wall, old-fashioned clocks from different time zones. Modern, corky, antique and new generation. Fancy furniture that gave a creative art look; 10 feet tall bookshelf filled with books, magazines and other old articles. Drops cell phone on the floor. Boom! "This is a really nice place! I've always felt curious about coming inside such an amazing place."

Sickle Cell Diseases in the Older Adult by Mya S Thien et al. Pathology. January 2017. Sickle Cell Disease (SCD) is an inherited hemoglobin disorder, associated with recurrent painful episodes, ongoing hemolytic anemia and progressive multi-organ damage. Until the early 1990's, survival beyond the fourth decade for a patient with SCD was considered unusual and prompted case reports. Nowadays, in countries with developed health care systems, more than 90 percent of newborns with SCD survive into adulthood. Nevertheless, their life expectancy, SCD has now evolved into a debilitating disorder with substantial morbidity resulting from ongoing sickle cell vasculopathy and multi-organ damage. Limited data on health care issues of older adults with SCD poses multiple challenges to patients, their families and health care providers. How I Treat the Older Adult with Sickle Cell Disease by Swee Lay Thein et al. Blood. 2018 with increasing survival, cumulative complications of sickle cell disease (SCD), which develop insidiously over time, are becoming more apparent and common in older patients, particularly those in their fifth decade and beyond. The older patient is also more likely to develop other age-related non sickle conditions that interact and add to the disease morbidity. A common misconception is that any symptom in a SCD patient is attributable to their SCD and this may lead to delays in diagnosis and appropriate intervention.

We recommend regular comprehensive reviews and monitoring for early signs of organ damage and a low threshold for the use of hydroxyurea and blood transfusions as preventative measures for end-organ disease. Treatable comorbidities and acute deterioration should be managed aggressively. Kim is hanging out with some of her friends as they sit together for some Netflix and popcorn. She wore a red jacket, long hair with braids going straight down. Black Nike gym shoe sneakers, caramel skin complexion. Long beautiful eye-lashes, sandy brown hair. Kim had on red pants, black Mickey Mouse t-shirt, small petite girl that weighed 113 lbs 5'3 feet tall. They were having a good time with her and the other two girls that are close. Barbie doll toys lay on the brown wooden floor next to the baby doll; Kim was looking over at the clock that stood out with the huge crack in the middle. "This is the best sleepover ever!" (Laughter) Kim's friend Becca shouts excitedly. "I'm literally thinking of colors to paint my nails." Kim's friend shouts out loud. "What color did you have in mind?" Kim looks over at the dresser with varieties of nail polish. "OH MY GOSH!" Kim's shouts! "You have a lot of nail polish." Kim's friend Becca says sarcastically. "What ten?!" "LOL, that's not a lot!" With laughter! "Girl!" Kim says to her friend Becca in a sense of humor. "You should paint them lime green. That would look pretty on you." With a smile, Kim says. Pointing her finger over at the nail polish. "Or purple for royalty." Kim says in a happy manner.

"Fine I'll paint them purple instead." Kim's friend Becca finally made up her mind and decided. Melissa came running into the room from outside where she was jump roping with the neighbor's daughter. "Hey guys how are you?" Out of breath. "Hey girl! Where were you?!" Shouts Kim and Melissa. "I was out front playing jump rope with the girl next door." As Becca explained. "You've made us worried! Thought you had got lost or kidnapped by a creep!" Says Kim sarcastically. "Oh no! Now I'm into Martial arts. That would never happen." Becca said in a serious manner to Kim and Melissa. "Should I put a pizza in the oven?" Are you guy's hungry!?" Smiling with high enthusiasm in her voice."YES! Pizza." Shouts Becca. "Actually, let's just get ready for bed. It's pretty late and my parents are sleeping. They have work tomorrow in the morning." Melissa says to her two friends as Kim was on her way into the kitchen. "Fine!" Kim looks at the refrigerator. "I am tired." Becca grabs the air mattress inside of the closet while she asks Melissa for a blanket. "Good night I love you guys." Melissa says to her friends Kim and Becca. "We love you more!" Kim, Becca hugs Melissa tight with genuine comfort. "Good night!" Smiling as the girls get ready for bed. Melissa turns off the night light in her bedroom. "See ya girls in the a.m." Melissa says, fixing her pillow. You could hear the birds chirping outside of the dawn atmosphere, communicating with each other. The rooster from down the block just near Melissa home was going off loud! Waking up the majority of the block.

That early morning Kim receives a call from her mother Debra to check up on her while she was out with her friends during their sleepover. (RING, RING, RING, RING) The phone begins to ring constantly waking Kim and her two friends Melissa, Becca up. "Sorry, it's my mom. Kim picks up the phone and is still half asleep. "Hey mom good morning." Debra says back quietly. "Good morning baby! I'm sorry for calling you so early. I just wanted to remind you don't forget to take your medicine and call me whenever you wake up." Yawning and talking as she sounded really tired. "I know what mom I want, I promise, and I will talk to you when I wake up. I love you Mama." Falling back to sleep. "I love you more baby talk to you later." Debra hangs up the phone slowly. As Mysteriously eccentric and elegant she could be, Debra wore a long black trench coat, purple high leather heels, a grey sweatshirt, with black jeans. Dark black and brown French braids, caramel melanin skin with long eyelashes. She was slim body shaped, brown eyes and her purple purse that Debra kept with her about 5"4 feet tall weighed 13lbs.

Chapter 6
Fatimah's Story

When both of Fatimah's parents were found to have the sickle cell trait (SCT), the possibility of their children having sickle cell disease (SCD) was a significant concern. As fate would have it, both Fatimah and her older sister were born with SCD, creating a challenging dynamic for their family. While her older sister's experience with the disease involved occasional pain crises, Fatimah faced more severe health complications, including frequent hospitalizations and debilitating pain episodes that impacted her daily life.

At the tender age of seven, Fatimah suffered a stroke that left her hospitalized for several months. Despite this traumatic event, she miraculously recovered, defying the odds and demonstrating remarkable resilience. Throughout her childhood, she grappled with the realization that her health struggles were different from those of her peers, making her journey a unique one. Despite the limitations imposed by her condition, Fatimah never allowed SCD to define her identity or dictate her aspirations. Her determination and perseverance served as an inspiration to her older sister, who was motivated to pursue a career in hematology and sickle cell research.

As she progressed into her college years, Fatimah decided to study abroad in Milan, Italy, despite her parents' concerns about her health management. Although she faced numerous challenges in navigating a foreign healthcare system, her indomitable spirit and positive mindset guided her through the experience, allowing her to cherish the moments and opportunities that came her way. Currently on the cusp of graduating as a finance major, Fatimah has secured a full-time position at JP Morgan Chase and remains dedicated to pursuing her interests in travel, blogging, and fashion. Her journey serves as a testament to the notion that individuals with SCD can lead fulfilling lives and achieve their dreams, notwithstanding the challenges they face.

As she progressed into her college years, Fatimah decided to study abroad in Milan, Italy, despite her parents' concerns about her health management. Although she faced numerous challenges in navigating a foreign healthcare system, her indomitable spirit and positive mindset guided her through the experience, allowing her to cherish the moments and opportunities that came her way. Currently on the cusp of graduating as a finance major, Fatimah has secured a full-time position at JP Morgan Chase and remains dedicated to pursuing her interests in travel, blogging, and fashion. Her journey serves as a testament to the notion that individuals with SCD can lead fulfilling lives and achieve their dreams, notwithstanding the challenges they face.

Chapter 7

Stumbling toward the door, Sam arrived home after an evening of unusual drinking, prompting concern from his wife, Debra. Clad in a casual ensemble, Sam's weary countenance concealed the strains of the day. Meanwhile, Debra, having returned from her errands, checked in on their daughter, Kim, recalling her recent complaints about chest pains and the challenges of finding a doctor who understood her condition. As Kim grappled with her sickle cell disease, her passion for singing and performing remained undeterred, fueled by her parents' unwavering support and encouragement.

Despite the hardships posed by her illness, Kim's determination and resilience shone through, drawing inspiration from her circle of friends and her unwavering commitment to her musical aspirations. With each visit to the hospital and each instance of battling medical professionals who didn't comprehend her condition, Kim's resolve only grew stronger, propelling her toward her dreams. As Debra and Sam shared intimate moments in the living room, discussing Kim's vocal class for the following day, their affectionate banter and playful exchanges added a touch of warmth to the ambiance. Kim's determination to pursue her singing career, irrespective of the limitations imposed by her health, underscored her unwavering spirit and determination.

In the midst of their family dynamics, the cultural nuances of their neighborhood in Chicago subtly found their way into the narrative, highlighting the community's unique cultural influences and societal expressions. Debra's conversation with Kim about her future endeavors and the significance of family values further emphasized the family's strong bond and shared aspirations. With dinner preparations underway, the kitchen became a hub of activity, resonating with the aromas of home-cooked soul food. Debra's culinary expertise, coupled with her motherly advice to Kim, added an endearing touch to the family's shared experiences. Sam's arrival and his affectionate acknowledgment of his cherished family members further underscored the family's deep-seated love and solidarity.

Sam struggles to get the key into the door he finally makes it inside. Being a person that dresses casually Sam wore a blue jean jacket, white t-shirt, white sneakers, and a long goatee beard. Afro from the 70's; brown corduroy pants. With blue matching socks. He carried his quill pen with Lean and muscular about 6"0 feet tall and weighed 185 pounds. "Okay let me get in the shower and wake myself up." Sam calmly said to himself. Debra just came in from being out running some errands since early that morning. As she made sure to check in on her daughter Kim, remembering when Kim told her that her chest was hurting while she was trying to rest. Which would cause her to go to the hospital. Kim would get very emotional due to her having a hard time getting the right doctor to really understand. "Hey baby, it's me!" Debra shouts towards the hallway. "Kim is doing great having fun with her friends Melissa and Becca." That's great honey, I'm happy to hear that."

Getting out of the shower, grabbing the towel. Sam practices gratitude everyday, always sending out abundance, opportunities, and success. Showing positivity towards others especially when he has a child to support and make sure she is on track with her health. Kim was a singer who was always putting on a show, entertaining her parents. Singing and dancing her father Sam takes her to vocal class, nothing is getting in the way of Kim going for her singing career. The older Kim got while dealing with her sickle cell disease she knew nothing could stop her from going after her passion. Not trying to fit in with the norms instead she goes all in and dive into her abilities. Staying in and out of the hospital has made her even stronger. Her friends even knew that Kim was up for greatness when it came to singing ever since she was a little girl. Sam and Debra were in the living room watching television and eating some snacks, "tomorrow I have to go pick up Kim. She has vocal class." Debra says to Sam.

"Okay honey that's fine, do you need me to go get her instead or you got it?" Sam says while drinking his Gatorade. "I got it, I will go get her, you can drop her off to her vocal class instead." Smiling at her husband Sam says Debra. "Does that sound fair enough?" Corouding biting his lips. "Yes, absolutely! I love it when you talk sexy to me like that." Sam says to his wife Debra as he slowly walks up to her and gently places his hand on her hips. "Yes, that feels so good when you touch me there." Debra says she is leaving with chills running through her body. Kissing in the living room by the front door, "Okay baby, I must go and get Kim now." Opens the door. Debra leaves out on her way to go pick up their daughter Kim from her friend's house. Kim will end up going to the hospital over and over due to her sickle cell disease. Putting on a fight with doctors and nurses that didn't quite understand because it was rare that the disease was even mentioned! Majority in the African American community are mostly blacks, or Hispanics, Asia and I'm sure so on anonymously. Kim always wanted to do the natural activities as the other people which involve hobbies like swimming and volleyball. Although, her passion was always singing and entertaining. At age 12 Kim was already active and doing fun activities. She knew her singing was going to take her somewhere; to a place she has never been.

Still being able to hang out with her friends, battling sickle cell anemia and traveling on tour. Debra finally arrives at Kim's friend's place. Honks the horn. Screaming out of the car. "KIM! I'm outside!" Kim and her friends Melissa, Becca shockingly jumped. Racing over to the window. "Look!" Shouts Becca. "I know it's my mom coming to pick me up." With a sad expression on her face Kim gathered her belongings, kissed and hugged her friends goodbye as she headed towards the door. "Hey, sweetie, how are you?" Debra is smiling at her daughter Kim. "I'm doing fine mom, thank you for asking." Says Kim. "Good! I love that." "We are cooking dinner tonight, your favorite soul food. Mac and Cheese, corn bread, baked chicken, BBQ baked chicken, cole slaw, stream beans, mash potatoes, and corn beef." Explaining all types of delicious soul food cooking Debra expresses how much of a passion to her daughter on how much she loves to cook. Especially when it comes to her family. They finally arrive home as they pull up to their place a group of guys was walking past one of them was just standing out in the middle of the street being obnoxious causing a scene. Pants hanging down showing their underwear. "Just a typical nigga." Debra says tirelessly. Shaking her head as she and Kim go inside.

Chicago is always known for having the gangster's, wanna be gangstas and thugs. Being a cultural based thing sagging your pants and wearing them down to your ankles was apparently a form of fashion, style, and slang. It became popular in the 1990s and the style was popularized by skaters and hip-hop artists in the 1990s. It later became a symbol of freedom and cultural awareness among some youths or a symbol of their rejection of the values of mainstream society. Debra starts to cook dinner and while preparing she was talking to Kim; her daughter about touring for singing. Her little pop star is soon to be in front of millions of people. Having all the support she possibly could have while pursuing her singing career. Chop up the onion on the slice board. Debra looks over her right and reaches for the other sharp knife. "Now this is why mama must always stay in the kitchen!" Debra says to Kim with a smile on her face of happiness and joy. "Someday Kim you will meet an attractive man that will come into your life, you may have beautiful children, house, car and all of the above. Debra explains while cooking to her daughter Kim. And then, you may become a wife to your fiancé! He would love for you to cook dinner while he goes out and provide the way your father does."

Kim was looking at her mother with a look of "aww" in her facial expression. Kim says to her mother Debra. "I would love that mom and someday to become a wife to the man of my dreams! Depending on the circumstances I would go by the morals that you and dad taught me, I will clean, cook and make sure the house is organized hahahaha!" They both laughed while continuing to multitask and work together simultaneously. Sam comes into the kitchen whistling. "My two beautiful ladies that I truly adore. It Smells good here." Sam says to his wife Debra and his daughter Kim. "Yes honey thank you! This is what we do!" glancing over at Kim with a grin. "I know. That's why I love you both!" Sam goes back into the living room continuing to watch his favorite movie on HBO.

Chapter 8
Sickle Cell Anemia Prevalent Among African Americans
Posted by nnlm scr on February 8th, 2018 Posted in: Blog.

With February being African American History Month, the focus of the blog shifts to health issues unique or more likely to impact African Americans. Among these diseases is sickle cell anemia, a condition found in about 1 in 13 African American births. MedlinePlus defines sickle cell anemia as a disease in which the body produces abnormally shaped red blood cells, leading to anemia and possible complications due to blood vessel blockages. The National Heart, Lung, and Blood Institute emphasizes the mandatory screening of all newborns in the United States, the District of Columbia, and U.S. territories for SCD, as the symptoms typically manifest after 5 or 6 months of age.

As the family continues to rally around Kim, Debra delves into comprehensive research on the Dr. Buteyko method, seeking to understand its potential in addressing oxygenation for chronic diseases like sickle cell anemia. Amidst her exploration of possible natural remedies, Debra's commitment to her daughter's health remains unwavering, and she rushes to Kim's aid during a severe sickle cell crisis. Despite the challenges, the family remains united in their support for Kim's well-being.

With Kim's dedication to her singing career taking her on tour, her parents grapple with the ongoing health concerns, striving to ensure her safety and comfort. Despite the setbacks, Kim's determination shines through, driving her to put on electrifying performances and connect with fellow artists, making the most of her time on stage.

As a sickle cell crisis lands Kim in the hospital during her tour, her parents receive the distressing call, prompting a hasty decision to travel to Jackson-Madison County General Hospital. Determined to be by their daughter's side, Debra and Sam swiftly prepare for the journey, opting to fly to Tennessee to ensure a timely arrival. Amidst the hustle and bustle of travel preparations, emotions run high, and the couple's unwavering love for their daughter serves as a guiding light in the face of uncertainty.

Rushing towards the door out of rage. Debra quickly tries to get her daughter Kim while she is having a scary sickle cell crisis.

"Baby! Are you okay?! Debra shouts at Kim. Where is your dad?!" Looking towards the window. "He's sleeping. Kim says. My chest just hurts really bad! And my arm." Kim laying down on the couch in the living room. "I will get you to the emergency room!" Debra takes Kim to the Hospital knowing that they're going to keep her for a couple days. Although Kim is resting in the hospital, Debra brings Dr. Buteyko to her husband Sam and shares tips and methods they can use for Kim to help her cure her sickle cell disease naturally. "We will have to form the Dr. Buteyko method on Kim especially, if she has another crisis." Debra explains to her husband Sam.

    A day goes by while Kim is in the hospital. She has a tour coming up in a few weeks and she is going through a tough moment. Singing and her vocal classes, Kim's instructor understood her problem and what she was going through. Meanwhile, her parents gathered as much information as possible to figure things out as long as Kim's health did not give up. It was sunny outside, about 60 degrees. Kim got out of the hospital, and she was getting ready to prepare herself to go on touring for singing. She had a show in Atlanta at an old auditorium, the total number of people showing up was 50. And they were cheering, shouting, and putting on a high vibrational enthusiasm during Kim's performance made her even more happier and confident.

    Putting on a great show in Atlanta was one of her most exciting moments. Getting ready for nationals out in Tennessee at a high school. Kim had to make sure that she was well rested, taking her medicine, and is feeling great. Her mother and father made it seem obvious on how strict they are due to their daughter having a crisis at any time, second, or minute. Going back out on stage Kim performed another great song of her collections, making the crowd interact with her music. Kim definitely puts on a show with such art, passion, and energy. The show is over! Kim ended her performance with a bang. Her crowd and the amount of energy in the room was amazing. Kim and her crew leave as they gather up on the tour bus. While on tour Kim has another sickle cell crisis after she finished performing for the nationals. Kim went backstage to take a break to get some water. She had put on a great show and felt very accomplished, and proud of herself. When Kim goes away on tour and travels to different cities, states her parents do not go; they cannot travel on their tour bus. So they just stay home anyway and watch her perform but television.

Debra, Sam, and Kim all understand that they're in two different states from each other. Performing two of her most popular songs ``Don't cry girl" and "I love you" her first song that she'd performed was "Don't cry girl" a song that Kim wrote when she was 10 years old. Now she is touring, traveling, and performing in front of many, many people. Perfecting her craft, promoting and networking at age 13. Very talented and creative she was getting all of the attention that she could get. Meanwhile, on tour she was able to meet some of the other greatest musicians and artists that made it big into Hollywood. Justin Beiber, Usher, Bow Wow, Billie Ellish, Chance The Rapper, Selena Gomez, Miley Cyrus, Vanessa Hudges, Jake Cyrus. Actor "Here comes the boom."Jackie Evancho self America's Got Talent, Malik Sosho dancer and choreographer of The Future Kingz TFK, Isiah Sosho leader and choreographer of The Future Kingz TFK, Bruno Mars. Soundtrack Rio 2, Adele. Soundtrack Skyfall. Chris Brown. Actor in the movie Takers and more.

After Kim's performance she had gone into a crisis while on tour with her crew and the camera guy. Her photographer rushed over to Kim where she was experiencing pain in her chest, arm, and made Kim have a horrible headache. "Oh my gosh! Kim, are you okay?!" Panicking out of breath while picking her up from off the floor. She had collapsed and been rushed to the hospital of Jackson-Madison County General located in Jackson Tennessee. When Kim and her singing crew had arrived at the Jackson-Madison County General Hospital they immediately called Kim's parents. The first ring no one had picked up they're guessing or assuming they did not recognize a number coming from another state, city from Chicago Illinois. The phone began to ring until someone picked up. Finally, Kim's father Sam answered the phone with a high pitched tone in his voice. "Yes! Hello, may I ask who's calling?!" The doctor from where the receptionist desk was near the drinking fountain had said and addressed that they're daughter Kim had a sickle cell crisis during her moment of anemia which can cause depending on the immunity of that particular individual system she couldn't handle the cold auditorium which triggered her sickle cell anemia.

"Right now we have her laying comfortably with a heated pad under her body to help her muscles relax. She doesn't have swelling or anything in particular that's going on." Sam told his wife Debra about the whole situation with their daughter's sickle cell crisis that

that took place while Kim was on tour. "Hey, honey just received a call from Jackson-Madison County General Hospital and they explained Kim had another crisis while on tour after she had finished performing." Debra walks closely up to her husband Sam with a surprisingly shocking look of worry in her face. "What! Really?" Debra shouts to Sam. "Yes! I know we must take that trip down to Jackson Tennessee. That way we can go pick up our daughter." "Okay we can do that, let's get up early tomorrow morning to go and pick up Kim." With a sense of humor Debra says calmly. "Are you okay with taking that drive? Or should I start looking up plane tickets?" Opening up his laptop Sam immediately starts searching for cheap affordable prices for travel. Points at the window, Debra asked Sam. "How long do you think it would take for us to drive down there?" Sam looks over at his cell phone and searches for the GPS. "About 7h 38min (484.6 mi)." Sam explained. "Really not that bad of a drive honey either way we gotta get there." With a look of aww. "I understand! Let's just take the plane instead. That way we will arrive a lot quicker." Debra says to her husband Sam.

   Gathering a few items to take with them during their travel flight towards Jackson-Madison County General Hospital. "Cell phone" Debra grabbing her bag and jacket; "drinking beverages? snacks, and keys, make sure you turn out the lights in the room's and kitchen, keep the lights on in the living room please!" On their way while driving to the O'Hare airport Debra and Sam stopped to get gas for when they get back home in Chicago, they want to worry about not getting to their destination in time. It's a chance that Kim possibly had to be home resting, taking her medicine her doctor had prescribed her with to help cope with her pain while she goes through a crisis. Debra and her husband Sam finally arrive at the airport. Running inside with their baggage to get a good position in line Debra starts crying overwhelmed with so many emotions due to her daughter Kim sickle cell anemia. Placing luggage on the floor Sam hugs his wife Debra tight. "It's going to be just fine baby, God is with us and our daughter; and Kim is a strong young lady." "Please don't cry love." Wiping her tears away with a tissue. "I love you honey." Debra says aloud to Sam, leaving passengers, travel agents etc in shock. Getting on the plane heading towards Jackson Tennessee it seems crowded with passengers and somewhat peacefully quiet, people relaxing listening to their music, watching movies on their portable device, eating, drinking and enjoying the flight.

Sam observes everyone that he sees on the plane thinking about the movies he watches on television showing a person acting out crazy, bizarre and creating terrorist threats he made sure that himself and including his wife Debra was safe and sound until they made it towards Jackson Tennessee. Born in Chicago, Illinois Sam was all about safety due to the environment that he grew up in. Especially when it came to his family, people and planes. Looking over to his right out of the window he sees the white clouds and light blue sky which amazed him while his wife Debra near the window dozes off peacefully asleep. He knew God was with them then. Yawning as he looks around again Sam goes to sleep until they make it. Passengers scream as the airplane turbulence while on the rise scares other passengers out of their sleep. Debra and Sam remain asleep, as if they couldn't feel turbulence. Pilot made a clear announcement saying "everything is alright ladies and gentlemen were going through the clouds." "Continue to relax, and enjoy the flight."

Chapter 9

McKeller-Sipes Regional Airport welcomed Debra and Sam to Jackson, Tennessee, where they unexpectedly encountered former NFL player Tiki Barber, who shared a similar struggle with sickle cell disease. Tiki Barber, a celebrated athlete, had risen to prominence during his time with the New York Giants. While dealing with Kim's illness and its repercussions, her parents grappled with the startling revelation of her addiction to pain medication, a concern that weighed heavily on their hearts. As the family reunited at the hospital, the emotional reunion brought tears of joy, reaffirming their unwavering love and commitment to Kim's well-being. Setting aside their worries for a moment, they savored the precious time together, cherishing every smile and hug that brought them closer.

Sam and Debra's unwavering support for Kim was further exemplified as they made their way to the airport, en route to their home in Chicago. Despite the challenges they faced, the couple's determination and resilience continued to shine through, providing an anchor of strength for their daughter. Throughout the journey, they strove to ensure Kim's comfort, safety, and happiness, going above and beyond to protect her from any harm. In the bustling airport, the Davis family encountered an eclectic mix of individuals, including a variety of individuals involved in illicit activities. The bustling airport terminal was a microcosm of diverse characters, with each person carrying their own story and struggles. However, amidst the chaos, the family focused on their unity and the love that bound them together, weathering any storm that came their way.

Boarding the flight back to Chicago, Debra's request for wine during the flight underscored the family's need for a moment of relaxation and relief. As they settled into their seats, the anticipation of returning home and the hope for a better tomorrow provided a glimmer of comfort, fueling their determination to overcome any obstacle that lay ahead. Kim was addicted to pain medication that her doctor has kept prescribing her with, which caused Kim at age 11 to keep taking medication just to absorb the high dosage of hydrocodone, oxycodone acetaminophen, and morphine. Kim was taking 5-10 pills a day even when she felt that her body didn't even need it, the fact is she just was addicted. The medication made her feel good and too young to be under the influence of a strong drug. It always brought tears to her parents' eyes and they felt like there was nothing to do. They understood that it was helping her cope with sickle cell anemia.

Leaving from the McKeller-Sipes Regional Airport on their way to the Jackson-Madison County General Hospital; Sam and Debra both were relieved and happy about going to pick up their daughter Kim while missing her while she was on tour singing. They went up to the receptionist desk to ask where they're daughter Kim was as they seemed excited and anxious. "Hello, my name is Debra Davis and this is my husband Sam Davis. We are here to pick up our daughter Kim Davis. May you help us find out what room she is in please?" Standing with her hands on her hips. The receptionist lady stood up from out of her seat and said follow me. "Yes, absolutely follow me this way." As they head over to the elevator going to the 4th floor where sickle cell patience was stationed. The receptionist lady said nicely. "Kim would be right in this room here room 206." Smiling at her husband and the receptionist lady. "You're the best! God bless you and we appreciate you so much for helping us." Debra said. "Yes my pleasure, is there anything else that I could possibly help or assist you with?" Ask the receptionist lady. "No, thank you we got it." Sam says appreciatively. "Great!" The receptionist lady takes off.

Debra and Sam push the door open quietly trying not to make noise waking the other patient that shared the same room with Kim. As they entered the room Kim was sleeping peacefully. Wipes her face. "Look at our beautiful daughter just sleeping peacefully." Debra mentions her husband Sam. "Yes she is resting greatly, let's stay here for another hour before we wake her baby." Sam says out of clarity. "Okay we could do that." Debra sits down next to Kim rubbing her long soft, curly hair. "That would be great! That would be great!" Pulling out his crossword puzzle with his yellow highlight sharpie to keep himself occupied, Sam was at ease. Kim finally wakes up looking shocked at her parents. Kim rubbing her eyes and stretching. "Hey mom. Hey dad." Debra and Sam both start smiling with such love and joy. "My baby! Sam shouts. I miss you so much!" Debra hugs Kim tight. Kim with all love, hugs, and kisses in her life intels happiness. The family gets ready to head out at a nearby hotel suite until the morning Sam booked their ticket back to Chicago.

Sam, Debra, and Kim had to be at the McKeller-Sipes Regional Airport by 8:30 AM for their flight that takes off at 9:08 AM.

Making a quick stop as they address the taxi driver to stop just one last time. Possibly making more than one stop than usual causing Sam to pay more cash that he barely had. This time the taxi driver did the family another last favor by making another stop to McDonalds to grab something to eat. Sam desperately shouts. "Please just this last time! Just do it for my family. My daughter has sickle cell anemia disease which causes her to stay back and forth at the hospital going through a bad crisis, they're hungry. Is that okay!? May you do that for me!?" The taxi driver can just feel the energy and the sadness running in their faces as he turns down his Latino music playing on the radio. "Okay! Okay! Amigo! I understand." They arrive at McDonalds Sam makes their order. "May I have a large Frie, small chocolate milk shake, four double cheese burgers, small orange juice, a little ice please, medium sprite, and another medium sprite!, three hash browns, a pack of BBQ sauce. That would be all." As Sam completes his order. The cashier lady shouts. " Your total would be $7.86." Sam hands over a ten dollar bill. "Here ten." The cashier lady hands back over to Sam his change and yells ``would you like the receipt "Hey would you like your receipt?" Sam looked at the taxi cab driver as if he was about to drive off. "No, thank you."

  The taxi driver took Sam and his family to the hotel suite free of no charge. "Thank you!" As the family thanked the taxi driver dearly. "No, problem." Sam and Debra made sure that their daughter Kim was safe, comfortable, and loved. That was the only strict boundary and commitment they had within themselves. Not only have they protected and supported Kim all through her sickle cell anemia disease as staying the strong parents, resilience, and hero. Due to Kim being the only child somewhere in her genetics one of her family members has sickle cell anemia or the trait. Her parents spoil her by shopping for her constantly, getting her what they call the best of what they can do. Taking care of her while she goes on her singing journey. Kim's perception of life and of was so unimaginable that most thought she was older. At a maturity level which made her stand out from the rest. And focused on her passion that made her purpose fulfill. Debra wanted to share something very exciting to both her husband and daughter's attention with a poem from The Best Poems Ever, a collection of poetry's greatest voices Edited by Edric S. Mesmer. "I would like to dedicate a famous poem written by Edna St. Vincent Millay to our daughter Kim."

Travel

The railroad track is miles away,
And the day is loud with voices speaking,
Yet there isn't a train goes by all day
But I hear its whistle shrieking.

All night there isn't a train goes by,
Though the night is still for sleep and dreaming,
But I see its cinders red on the sky,
And hear its engine steaming.

My heart is warm with the friends I make,
And better friends I'll not be knowing;
Yet there isn't a train I wouldn't take,
No matter where it's going.

  Sam and Kim were both in awe; they loved every bit of it with care and understanding. Thinking to themselves "makes sense" and describing the reality of what most live. The first thing that came to Kim was "travel" and that is what she did. Going on tour for singing, talent shows and competitions, fun rallies, local shows. To sum it up about how much she'd loved the poem that was said from her mother Debra. Written by Edna St. Vincent Millay, one of her mother's favorites, growing up in elementary school with only five other black African American in her class herself, a girl and three boys that hardly paid attention in class to the teacher. Always goofing around, being obnoxious, disrupting the classroom rules. Debra started to have memories of when she was in school on the cheerleading team. Majority of her husband Sam's side of the family is from the Southside Lowend of Chicago, some of his relatives live in Englewood and went to Simeon Career Academy for sports, academics and cold hard talent.
  They both love their culture and city, getting ready for bed so they can wake up in the morning to catch their flight back to Chicago. Meanwhile Kim is feeling a lot better especially when both of her parents came to support her. Tuesday morning the family gets ready in head towards the McKeller-Sipes Regional Airport on their way home back to Chicago it was a sunny day outside; all the Dallas hustlers, and pimps was out in their fancy cars with exoctic woman

one of the pimps had leashes attached to the woman showing control, power, and dominance. Prostitutes, escorts, private individuals that sold themselves for money, power, and greed seem to be roaming the airport. Security guards knew what they were up to. They just didn't bother the pimps and hustlers only if they felt threatening and something was happening to an extreme. Other than that, everyone kept their composure and was just hanging out until they were told to move away from the facility although, the pimps had some type of self-respect when it came to the senior citizens that were at the airport staying out of their way which seemed odd and out of the ordinary. You can tell that some of the hardcore pimps grew up with some type of manners, boundaries, and understanding when it came to their elders.

The love for money didn't stop them from making money and provoking these woman of innocence and guilt go out and make a profit by pleasing married men, single men, any male that had a thing for these certain type of woman if they're not getting any attention from their wives or the men simply wanted to have experience with prostitutes along while they're wife is home with their children. Spending big bucks doing drugs and alcohol living that lifestyle as if nothing else even matters. All types of different races, whites, black, Indian, Hispanic, Latino, Latin were all satisfying their clients' needs and wants. Prostitution has been practiced throughout ancient and modern culture. Prostitution has been described as "the world's oldest profession," and despite consistent attempts at regulation, it continues nearly unchanged. Example: In New York, prostitution is treated as a misdemeanor punishable by up to three months in jail and a fine of up to $500. ... Nevada is the only U.S. state to allow some form of legal prostitution in certain counties through the operation of brothels. Flight attendant had made an announcement that seats will be available in 10 minutes.

As Kim, Debra, and Sam headed on the plane Debra asked one of the flight attendants if she could get served alcohol while on the plane. The flight attendant says aloud to all passengers, "please form a single file line to get on to the plane!" Debra tapped the flight attendant lady on her shoulder. "Excuse me, would it be possible if I can have some whine once we all get situated?" The lady responded with a look of exhaustion. "Yes, we will serve alcohol to all adults when the flight takes off. Does that sound fair enough? Debra excitedly replies, "yes that sounds amazing thank you!" Passengers remain in their seats before the plane takes off towards Chicago O'Hare announcements come on the anacon, "please be seated for all safety standards and flight purposes we'll be heading in Chicago within five minutes." Landing in Chicago at the O'Hare airport they gather up their belongings heading towards the car.

Chapter 10

Dr. Buteyko emphasized the importance of nasal breathing during exercise, warning that mouth breathing could significantly reduce CO_2 levels, diminishing the health benefits of physical activity. Deeply engrossed in the teachings of Dr. Buteyko and Dr. Artour Rakhimov, Debra delved deeper into the intricacies of their theories, absorbing the complexities of the relationship between negative emotions and the nervous system.

Recognizing the significance of various factors on respiratory health, Debra and Sam explored a multitude of techniques and postures, including the utilization of water procedures, massage, and specific yoga postures. As they delved into the physiological effects of breathing practices, they uncovered the nuanced nature of yogic breathing methods, clarifying that the seemingly deep breaths of yogis were, in fact, shallow breaths performed at a slow and controlled pace.

Understanding the intricacies of these techniques, Debra and Sam discerned the underlying physiological benefits derived from the reduction in respiration, reflecting on the wisdom and intelligence behind the yogic system. Disentangling the mystique surrounding the practices, they recognized the profound significance of controlled breathing as an essential pathway to achieving breathlessness and immortality, devoid of the misconceptions that had clouded its true essence.

Chapter 11

As a young girl coping with sickle cell disease, Kim found solace in activities like camping, discovering a sense of belonging and normalcy among other children facing similar challenges. Reflecting on her experiences, Kim reminisced about the joys of camp life, emphasizing the inclusive atmosphere and the range of exciting activities that brought camaraderie and joy to all the campers. Through engaging in various camp programs and educational sessions, Kim and her fellow campers learned valuable lessons on managing their condition, emphasizing the importance of hydration, healthy eating, and appropriate clothing to regulate body temperature and prevent overexertion. Drawing strength from the shared experiences at camp, Kim emphasized the empowering impact of participating in talent shows and other group activities, fostering a strong sense of identity and self-worth.

While grappling with her own health struggles, Kim received guidance and inspiration from her vocal teacher, Mr. Rogers, who provided invaluable advice for those living with sickle cell disease. Encouraging the formation of a supportive community and the understanding of individual triggers for sickle cell crises, Mr. Rogers emphasized the importance of mental health and self-advocacy in managing the condition. Recognizing the challenges faced by parents of children with sickle cell disease, Mr. Rogers highlighted the significance of nurturing independence and resilience in their children, encouraging them to explore and take calculated risks while providing a supportive and encouraging environment.

Despite the hardships and pain she endured, Kim remained determined and resilient, facing each day with strength and fortitude. Her struggles were a testament to her unwavering spirit and determination to overcome the challenges posed by her condition, serving as an inspiration to those around her. Kim opens up to her mother Debra as they have a serious conversation on her dealing with the disease. "Camp was a place I could go where I never felt alone. I was no longer the black sheep in my family. It was a way of just feeling normal. There were other people there who had sickle cell like me, some who went to the hospital more than me and some who went less often." Kim looking at her childhood pictures from years ago talking to her mother Debra. According to Kim, "anyone with sickle cell disease can attend camp, which lasts from Saturday to Saturday. It is an opportunity for kids to feel normal and get to know other people with the condition. There are so many fun things to do at camp, such as archery, horseback riding, swimming, campfires and songs, talent shows, and treasure hunts. In addition, the camps provide sickle cell educational programs, where they teach kids a number of things, including how to manage their condition, stay hydrated, eat healthy, dress appropriately to stay warm, and avoid over-exerting themselves.

Most kids tend to start camp when they are 7 or 8 years of age 14 or 15. Many are repeat campers." According to Kim, "once you have the camp experience, it is something you want to do again and again unless you get sick or move away." Keep fighting, keep going, and stay persistent. Attending sickle cell camp helps support young people living with the disease in a number of ways. First, it helps kids learn that they are not isolated and alone. Second, it gives kids a sense of self identity and value. It also helps build self esteem through activities such as the talent show, in which kids are able to perform in front of their peers and showcase what makes them unique, exposing campers to new things. Although, Kim was speaking with her singing teacher for vocal lessons. Mr. Rogers was also a fighter when it comes to sickle beta zero thalassemia or Hbs beta 0- thalassemia. When asked what tips he has for kids living with sickle cell disease, Mr. Rogers offered the following:

"Find your tribe. It will help give you the sense that you're not alone in this. It's like the Bible verse, "A cheerful spirit is the best medicine." Your mental health, in terms of depression and anxiety, makes the severity of sickle cell disease worse, so your tribe is huge. Know your sickle cell algorithm. In other words, know which factors (for example, cold or hot weather) can trigger a sickle cell crisis that are specific to your body and adjust and manage those. Transition should be a rite of passage for all young adults with sickle cell disease. It's more important than other rites of passage in a young adult's life, such as learning to drive, going to prom, and going to college. It's critical that you learn to make your own medical appointments. You have to be able to take care of yourself. Glancing down at his Gold Rolex watch, "Kim is a strong girl, this is something that I want for you and your husband Sam to know." When asked what advice he has for parents of kids living with sickle cell disease, Mr. Rogers offered the following.

"Learn to let go. Don't be fearful and overprotective. You want your child to not only survive, but to thrive on their own. Your child doesn't have to be defined by this. Be measured, know what their strengths and weaknesses are, and continue to challenge them." Encourage them to explore a bit and take some risks. Rocking back and forth, stiffness from head to toe. Kim was in pain most often due to the change of the weather, stress, trauma, depression and unhealthy eating habits. Kim's eyes would turn more yellowish as if she was having a crisis suffering from bad anxiety causing Kim to separate and become distant from others. Without any circumstances Kim kept on fighting, being strong. It was December 12th, very chilly and cold.

    The leaves were frosty causing the snow from the roof gutters to fall. Children outside building snowman's, and as snow angels running around the playground down the street from Sam's cousin's apartment on the north side of Chicago. The back door opened "yo! Where y'all at?" As Jackson walks inside shouting all loud and obnoxious. "I need you to run me to the liquor store." Sam places his hand on his forehead "come on cuz! There's going to be a snow blizzard here in about five minutes." Looking up at the sky "those kids are about to start heading back inside watch what I tell you." Jackson looked at the sky as something was about to fall from the sky into his hands. They both begin to chuckle heading back inside. Pouring a glass of water "if the snow storm doesn't arrive we'll head out then quickly; or better yet just give me ten minutes you lucky that you are my cousin, and I love you Jay!" Sam with a fondness demeanor. Chirping the key alarm to unlock the vehicle door. "You noticed how strong this wind is coming our way." Sam says to his cousin Jackson. Clicking his safety belt and adjusting his seat "it doesn't stop me from getting my drinky drink on ha! He'll I'm thirsty... why not" Jackson responded gracefully. Sam glanced over his right one hand on the steering wheel "you are one lucky son of a gun." Imagine how many people in this world could just have their way. I mean it's possible. Anything is possible.

Chapter 12

During a school music rehearsal, Kim experienced a painful sickle cell crisis, prompting her classmates and teachers to rally around her with various efforts to ease her discomfort. Observing Kim's need for warmth, the students provided blankets and a heating pad, demonstrating their compassion and concern for their friend's wellbeing. As Kim's vocal teacher, Mrs. Francis, and fellow musician Jack discussed ways to better support Kim, they emphasized the importance of maintaining a suitable body temperature and exploring potential solutions to help her manage her condition effectively. With a shared determination to find a solution, the two teachers recognized the significance of a collaborative effort in providing Kim with the care and support she needed.

Continuing their research on sickle cell anemia, the class delved into the realm of nutrition, identifying key healthy foods that could benefit individuals living with the condition. Through their investigation, they discovered the importance of incorporating sea moss, black seed oil, fruits, vegetables, and other natural supplements into a balanced diet. Recognizing the role of nutrients in supporting overall well-being, the teachers and students developed a comprehensive plan to enhance Kim's dietary intake and ensure she received the necessary nutrients to support her health. Exploring the reasons behind the prevalence of sickle cell disease in individuals of African heritage, the class uncovered the genetic underpinnings that contribute to the inheritance of the condition. With a better understanding of the genetic factors at play, they recognized the significance of awareness and education in addressing the challenges faced by individuals living with sickle cell disease.

Drawing upon their collective efforts, Mrs. Francis, Jack, and the class collaborated with a nutritionist to develop a tailored dietary plan for Kim. Through discussions with the nutritionist, they established a framework for incorporating nutritious foods, supplements, and exercise regimens to support Kim's overall wellbeing and health. With the support of the school community and the guidance of the nutritionist, Kim's family expressed their gratitude for the collective efforts aimed at improving Kim's quality of life and well-being.

Placing the book down flat on the table "hmm what would help

Kim cope better with her sickle cell." Mrs. Francis Kim's other vocal teacher asked, "Does Kim's body get cold? I wonder how's her temperature is like in different atmospheres." Mrs. Francis walked towards the desk. "Maybe we all could create a solid solution; the future is always bright!" Jack the singer with his hat spinning off of his hand "absolutely problems to all things can be solved, we as spiritual leaders have to make that happen." "Your answer is good enough." Says Mrs. Francis "how can we all get together on this?" "When can we all get together on this? When can we all get started finding more spiritual answers, sources from the spiritual world!" Response Jack the singer "aw you got it!" Says Mrs. Francis "I want you all to just please relax, I am fine." Kim stretches her arms out with great strength. "But we have to help you." Jack the singer says "there's no but thank you God for giving me courage, strength and faith." Kim softly speaks. "It's not for no reason it will help us stay more according to our word." Mrs. Francis and the rest of the teacher's response. Jack the singer scratching his forehead "she's in control" Mrs. Francis with a look of confusion "wait wha!?"

  What are some other good healthy foods those that suffer with Sickle Cell Anemia should take into consideration? Get plenty of calcium-rich foods and beverages such as milk, yogurt, and cheese. Let's dive deeper! Nutrition for the Child with Sickle Cell Anemia. Sickle cell anemia is associated with vitamin D deficiency and poor appetite. Both can lead to delayed growth and development in children and can result in a need for a higher amount of certain nutrients, including calories and protein. Vitamin D works with calcium to help your child build strong bones. Children with darker skin may be more likely to be vitamin D deficient. Discuss vitamin D with your child's healthcare provider and whether a supplement is needed. Calcium and vitamin D are important for a child's growth and development, but other nutrients are needed, too, so good overall nutrition is essential. Keep these tips in mind to maximize your child's nutrition:

  Make good nutrition a family affair so your child isn't left drinking milk while everyone else has a soft drink. Get plenty of calcium-rich foods as beverages such as milk, yogurt and cheese. Other sources of calcium include leafy green vegetables and calcium fortified products such as soy milk and tofu, as well as some types of breakfast cereals and 100% fruit juice. Provide nutrient-rich, nuts and nut butters, or smoothies if your child doesn't have much of an appetite. Sauces, gravies and sources of fat may also be added to meals and snacks for extra calories.

Encourage plenty of fluids, especially water, to help prevent dehydration and constipation. Forgo sugar-sweetened beverages for milk or calcium-fortified 100% orange juice, which provide essential nutrients to help with your child's growth. Understandably, it may be easier said than done. Busy families may find cooking at home to be challenging. Enjoying a meal together as a family is important, especially for a child with a chronic illness. Work with a registered dietitian nutritionist to better understand your child's unique nutrition needs and identify quick and healthy meals that will work for the entire family.

Why is sickle cell disease more common in children of African heritage? A carrier of a single hemoglobin S gene is said to have Sickle cell trait or hemoglobin S "trait". About 1 in 12 people of African ancestry carry the S trait. Sickle cell trait is also common in people with ancestors from the Caribbean, Latin America, Middle East, India, South America, Central America, and Mediterranean countries such as Turkey, Greece, and Italy. Sickle cell trait is found today in descendents of these populations no matter where they live. People with hemoglobin S trait alone do not have sickle cell disease. However, if their reproductive partner also has the hemoglobin S trait, then together they have a 1 in 4 chance (25%) of having a child with sickle cell disease. This is why even bi-racial and/or multi-racial children can have sickle cell disease; about 1 in 365 people of African ancestry have sickle cell disease.

Together the class came up with a great solution for Kim. Spending hours doing tons of research on sickle cell anemia disease both teacher's Mrs. Francis and Jack The Singer met up with a nutritionist going over the proper healthy diet for Kim. Excitingly throwing his hands up in the air with a cheerful enthusiasm. "That's it! Found a solution. I remember me, you and Kim's parents were speaking at one point." Jack The Singer explains to Mrs. Francis. Rushing towards the table pulling out her seat from underneath eager to hear more. "We can get Kim a nutritionist it will be worth it, I've already gotten the approval from Mrs. Debra and Mr. Sam. Seeking information and knowledge is key, this will help Kim with eating healthy, proper exercise, being more active while involving in different activities now we all know that it starts in the mind! We all know that having faith, courage, and discipline to maintain these protocols Kim's going to love this." Jack The Singer recalls. Arriving at his Nutritionist Anthony office Jack The Singer walks inside. Nutritionist gracefully explains to Jack The Singer on proper eating habits that are important for Kim. "Eating greens, leafy foods, vegetables and taking her supplements." The cell phone rings. Ring, ring, ring. In Jack's pocket receiving a call from Debra Kim's mother. "One moment this is Kim's mother Debra calling." Jack The Singer says to Anthony reaching his hand into his right sided pocket pulling his phone out.

"Hello, hey Debra, how are you?" Debra responded. "I'm feeling fantastic, blessed." Jack The Singer responded. "That's great!" Debra asked Jack if he ended up meeting with Kim's nutritionist. Debra excitedly asked Jack. "Have you spoken with Anthony?" Jack The Singer replied. "Yes I have, I'm actually with him now as we speak." With laughter. Debra excitedly says. "Oh exciting!" "Would you like to speak with Anthony?" Jack asks Debra. "Absolutely, I appreciate everything and all that you do." Debra's response. "Hey Anthony, how are you?" Debra asked Kim nutritionist. "I am wonderful, how can I help?" Anthony responded to Debra. Debra responded to Anthony. "I've noted everything that you guys came up with for my daughter Kim. It's an honor and blessing from Kim's teachers, classmates, everyone that came together and participated with a solution that would benefit and help us all. I just wanted to tell you all how much me and Kim's father Sam appreciate the support and couldn't do it without you guys! It's really going to help Kim." Anthony deliberately explained to Debra. "My pleasure please continue to go over a healthy diet for Kim, make sure she is getting in plenty of nutrients by taking her supplement vitamins such as vitamin D, plenty of calcium-rich foods and exercising." Anthony explained. "This routine is going to help Kim." Debra responded to both Jack The Singer, and Anthony as she got ready to hang up the phone. "Thank you so much! I am blessed to have such awesome teachers, and leaders in my life." Debra giving thanks and gratitude. Anthony hands over the phone back to Jack. "Thank you!" Anthony slowly headed out of his office where his home was located in a nice neighborhood. "Gratitude!" Jack The Singer replies gracefully. "I will talk with you soon Mrs. Debra, enjoy the rest of your day." The call ends.

Chapter 13

In the pursuit of addressing the complexities of sickle cell anemia, the narrative explores potential treatment options, including bone marrow transplants as a means of replacing affected bone marrow with healthy donor marrow. This usually takes place from a family relative or a sibling that has healthy blood cells. The discussion delves into the diagnostic processes for sickle cell disease, highlighting the importance of high-performance liquid chromatography (HPLC) and genetic testing in identifying the condition. The narrative further underscores the misconceptions= surrounding the capabilities of individuals living with sickle cell anemia, emphasizing their potential for various career paths and pursuits despite the challenges they face. However, it also sheds light on the behavioral and physical difficulties that can arise as a result of the disease, such as emotional struggles, pain-related issues, and challenges related to sexual health and physical mobility.

Exploring the impact of sickle cell disease on men and women, the narrative acknowledges the various complications that can arise, including issues related to puberty, fertility, and pain management. It elucidates the disparities in disease severity and life expectancy among individuals with different types of sickle cell disease, emphasizing the challenges and significant medical risks associated with the condition. The narrative delves into the experiences of individuals with sickle cell disease, highlighting the limitations and constraints they face in their daily lives. It also emphasizes the importance of effective pain management and supportive care, noting the crucial role that a comprehensive treatment plan and understanding medical professionals play in ensuring the well-being of those living with the disease.

As the story progresses, it follows Kim's journey towards comprehensive treatment and holistic care, focusing on her determination to pursue her passion for music while also prioritizing her health and well-being. The narrative captures the emotional struggles and challenges faced by Kim and her loved ones, underscoring the significance of a supportive community and empathetic medical professionals in facilitating her journey toward healing and improved quality of life.

How is the sickle cell test performed? The best way to check for sickle cell trait or sickle cell disease is to look at the blood using a method called high-performance liquid chromatography (HPLC). This test identifies which type of hemoglobin is present. To confirm the results of HPLC, a genetic test may be done. Most individuals that are born with sickle cell anemia think they can't or cannot do anything. Really all in reality they do! Many work from home jobs, in the healthcare field, YouTube channeling, trading or investing into the financial markets, and professional athletes. Anything they put they're minds toward. Stem cells are special cells produced by bone marrow, a spongy tissue found in the center of some bones. They can turn into different types of blood cells. What most did not know is that stem cell transplant is a possible restoration for sickle cell disease. It's usually considered only for children younger than sixteen who have severe complications from the disease. But they're not done very often because of the significant risk involved. Most people with sickle cell disease get really frustrated.

    This could cause bad behavior, anger issues, talking back with their parents, doctors, nurses, spouse, whoever it may be if you don't want to be in their way if anything try to help them cope better, offer support and show them that you care, and are there for them. Anyone could have a bad day or something had gone wrong in becoming off as aggressive. Those with sickle cell behavior patterns seem to be worse at dealing with such pain. Men that have sickle cell disorder discover bad erections, pain while urinating and more sexual dysfunction. Most young men with SCD eventually mature sexually. However, men with SCD are more likely to experience infertility because of hypogonadism (testosterone deficiency), sperm abnormalities, and erectile dysfunction. Up to 24 percent of adult men with SCD experience hypogonadism. Some men and women with the disease don't have any muscles so they can't walk or stand in proper position, or correct posture. Swelling in the body to a point where it will split through the layers of the skin. Causes an explosion to the veins in the hands, feet, toes, nail, legs, and the human body in overall. Men and women have similar rates of sickle cell disease (SCD). This is because SCD is not sex-linked. This means that the mutated gene in SCD is not on the sex chromosome. However, complications of SCD can affect men and women differently.

    In men, SCD can cause delayed puberty and issues having children. SCD can also block blood flow out of the penis. Also the men have SS sickle cell disease and SC which is worse and dangerous can kill you. They experience more excruciating pain and suffering when going through a crisis. Patients with Hb SC disease live longer than patients with Hb SS and have fewer painful episodes, but this disorder is associated with considerate morbidity and mortality, especially after age 30. Could take about 2-3 months until a patient experiences sickle cell crisis, a lot of them dying due to the Black disease. Doctors will have to sedate the patient. It's a serious disease mostly in African Americans. Most of them have to go to another emergency department. They don't always make it. Body deteriorates through a bad sickle cell crisis. People born with sickle cell can't barely enjoy themselves like others may do normally or on a daily basis. No drinking alcohol beverage's partying, accessing swimming pools, some things will be affected differently. It's a new day, it's a new life Kim is finally receiving the full treatment that she needed. Kim is able to cope with her sickle cell pain by eating more healthier, exercising more, stressing less and meeting new positive friends.

Kim even met a great gentleman that was her childhood best friend in the first grade at the time they are now moving on with something that is quite serious especially at their age. Focusing on her music and singing career which is Kim's passion. Healing, learning,= growing, and being more conscious towards her health. No more eating unhealthy foods, junk or drinking soda. Adding a healthy eating habit to her lifestyle has made it helpful for Kim. Even though Kim still goes through pain having a bad crisis which will draw her to cry out loud letting others around her know how serious the pain is. Being rushed to the hospital causes those around her to panic, especially her loved ones who know her really well. Kim would go days, months even weeks staying in the hospital until she feels better. Barely having the time and strength to spend the holidays with family and see friends Kim spends the majority of her life hospitalized. Going through a major sickle cell crisis switching from countless doctors, nurses and staff to really understand her pain. Kim's friends and family go to visit her while she is in the hospital. Her music teachers and classmates even come and visit her keeping Kim company making sure she is loved and doing alright.

As the snow began to melt down it was getting close to spring as nice weather was slowly approaching the Chicago land area. Kim went through a bad crisis where she had acute chest pains that caused her to get a blood transfusion to make her feel better. In spending more time in the hospital, some of the nurses, staff and NA's did not quite understand how to help Kim with her pain. Kim got so angry and frustrated she ended up calling the police while being at the hospital so they could take her pain more seriously. And the police officers were genuine and understanding of Kim's frustration. They knew that Kim was in a lot of pain. The officers told the nurse, doctors to take her sickle cell pain more seriously. It was a prejudiced moment against Kim that had received the most treatment and was understood. Kim was happy and felt safe being at the hospital on the second floor at the University of Chicago. Illinois seems to have great medical care and fully supportive staff, where a lot of sickle cell patients were treated properly with care.

....

Testimonial:

Hi, I'm Ollienna Ayanna Bluitt, and I'd like to share my journey with Sickle Cell Disease. On August 19, 1996, I was diagnosed with Sickle Cell Disease. It's been a challenging road for my parents, especially my mom. Despite my pain crises starting at the age of 4-6, my mom always took great care of me, ensuring I received the necessary treatment.

My mom's strength was truly remarkable, considering that my elder sister, Ivy Bluitt, 36, also battles with the same condition. However, with the grace of God, both my sister and I managed to lead fairly normal lives. My sister even has four kids of her own, and I was able to actively participate in sports during high school, go out with friends, and enjoy parties.

I've always refused to let Sickle Cell Disease define me because I believe in my inner and outer beauty. Now at 26, I continue to live the blessed life I've been given, even though I still face occasional pain crises. However, each battle only serves to make me stronger.

Made in the USA
Monee, IL
11 June 2024

59259325R00039